Carlo Cestra

The Japanese Battleship Musashi

KAGERO

The Battleship *Musashi*, 1944 – starboard side.

The *Musashi* battleship was the second ship of the Yamato class of Imperial Japanese Navy during the Second World War.

She and her sister, *Yamato*, were the heaviest and most powerful battleships ever constructed, displacing 72 800 tons at full load and armed with nine 46 cm Type 94 main guns.

***Musashi* was commissioned on August 1942 and assigned to the 1st Battleship Division. In early 1943 the ship was transferred to Truk, that was the Empire of Japan's main base in the South Pacific. During this year she sortied several times with the fleet searching for American forces, without success. In 1944 she was used to transfer forces and equipment between Japan and various occupied islands. In early 1944 she was damaged by an American submarine attack and was forced to return to Japan for repairs. On this occasion she was strongly enhanced with anti-aircraft armament. She was present during the Battle of the Philippine Sea in June, but she didn't engage in combat with the American forces.**

On 24 October 1944, during the Battle of Leyte Gulf, after several hours of fighting, *Musashi* was sunk by a large number of torpedos and bombs hit from the American carrier-based aircraft.

The wreck was located in March 2015 by the team of Microsoft co-founder Paul Allen, to a depth of about 1350 m (4430 feet).

Design

The Washington Treaty of 1922, with his prohibitions on the building of new battleships, held back Japanese projects for the development of the Fleet, which comprised the building of eight modern battlecruisers and eight modern battleships. The Japanese designers and engineers wished to build new high quality units. They considered the US Navy a potential opponent and wanted to ensure that their ship would be stronger and better armed than the US ships. Despite treaty prohibitions, the Bureau of Naval Construction carried on with their studies about the building of battleships and in 1930 they reached a new phase of development. In 1934 Japan withdrew from the League of Nations, renouncing its treaty obligations. In October 1934 the Bureau of Naval Construction received from the Naval General Staff the order to produce a design study of a new battleship with 46 cm guns and a speed of 30 knots. The vessels of the *Yamato* class were designed to be capable of engaging multiple enemy battleships at the same time.

After numerous tests and experiments, round large bulge was placed at the bow to reduce resistance and improve speed. A bulge of such a size and shape was unique at that time. In addition the hull had a shallow draught for a ship with such large displacement; so *Musashi*, and *Yamato* too, could use the naval base and dry docks of Imperial Japanese Navy as they was, without dredging or rebuilding. To increase the hull strength, and at the same time, reduce its weight, a new and innovative method was introduced. The armour plating was an integral part of the hull construction and not only an added protection. So the thickness and rigidity of the armour plating reinforced the hull strength too.

The characteristic shape of the stern resulted by the necessity of placing the hawse pipes away from the ship's centre line to protect the bulbous bow from anchors.

Boats, planes and other equipment were placed in protected magazines and hangars to protect them from being damaged by the terrific blast of the 46 cm guns. In fact the blast pressure of this weapon was capable of destroying boats or tearing the clothing from crew

Top view.

and making them unconscious. So ventilation openings were placed in strategic way to reduce or avoid the effect of the blast.

Musashi had a length of 244 m between perpendiculars and 263 m overall. She had a beam of 36.9 m and a draft of 10.86 m at deep load. She displaced 6 4000 long tons at standard load and about 72 000 tons at deep load. Her crew consisted of 2500 officers and men in 1942, and about 2800 in 1944.

She had four sets of Kampon geared steam turbines, each of which drove one propeller shaft. The turbines were designed to produce a total of 150 000 shat horsepower (11 0000 kW), using steam provided by 12 Kampon water-tube boilers, to give her a maximum speed of 27 knots (50 km/h). She had a storage capacity of 6300 long tons of fuel oil, giving her a range of 7200 nautical miles (13 300 km) at a speed of 16 knots (30 km/h)

Armour

The ship's waterline armour belt was 410 mm thick and angled outwards 20 degrees at the top. Below there was a strake of armour that ranged in thickness from 270 to 200 mm over the magazines and machinery spaces respectively; it tapered to a thickness of 75 mm at its bottom edge. The deck armour ranged in thickness from 230 to 200 mm. The turrets were protected with an armour of 650 mm thick on the face, 250 mm on the sides, and 270 mm on the roof. The barbettes of the turrets were protected by 560 to 280 mm thick armour, and the turrets of the 155 mm guns were protected by 50 mm armour plates. The sides of the conning tower were protected by 500 mm thick armour and the roof had a 200 mm thick plate. The floors of the ammunition magazines were protected by 50 to 80 mm armour plates which extended from the bottom of the magazines and across watertight compartments above the double bottom of the hull's shell; this would have protected the magazines from the explosion of a hostile torpedo or mine beneath the ship.

Musashi contained 1147 watertight compartments to preserve buoyancy in the event of battle damage.

Armament

The main battery consisted of nine 45 calibre 46 cm Type 94 guns mounted in three triple gun turrets, each with an elevation range of –5 to +45 degrees. They fired a 1460 kilogram armour-piercing (AP) shell to a range of 42 000 m. These were the largest calibre guns ever fitted to a ship. The guns had a rate of fire of 1.5 to 2 rounds per minute.

The ship's secondary battery consisted of twelve 60 calibre 15.5 cm 3rd Year Type guns mounted in four triple turrets, one each fore and aft of the superstructure and one on each side amidships. With a 55.87 kilograms AP shell, the guns had a maximum range of 27 400 m at an elevation of 45 degrees. Their rate of fire was five rounds per minute. Heavy anti-aircraft defence was provided by a dozen 40 calibre 127 mm Type 89 dual purpose guns in six twin turrets, three on each side of the superstructure. When firing at surface targets, the guns had a range of 14 700 m. They had a maximum ceiling of 9440 m at their maximum elevation of 90 degrees. Their maximum rate of fire was 14 rounds per minute. Their sustained rate of fire was around eight rounds per minute.

Musashi also carried thirty six 25 mm Type 96 light anti-aircraft (AA) guns in triple-gun mounts, all mounted on the superstructure. These 25 mm guns had an effective range of 1500–3000 m, and an

Port side view.

effective ceiling of 5500 m at an elevation of +85 degrees. The maximum effective rate of fire was only between 110 and 120 rounds per minute because of the frequent need to change the fifteen-round magazines. This was the standard Japanese light AA gun during World War II. It suffered from severe design shortcomings that rendered it a largely ineffective weapon. The ship was also provided with four 13.2 mm Type 93 anti-aircraft guns mounted on two twin gun turrets, one on each side of the bridge. The maximum range of these guns was 6500 m, but the effective range against aircraft was only 1000 m. The cyclic rate was adjustable between 425 and 475 rounds per minute. The need to change 30 round magazines reduced the effective rate to 250 rounds per minute.

While the ship was under repair in April 1944, the two 15.5 cm wing turrets were removed and replaced with three triple 25 mm gun mounts each. Twenty-one triple 25 mm mounts and 25 single mounts were added, for a total light AA armament of one hundred and thirty 25 mm guns.

Fire control and sensors

The ship was equipped with four 15 m rangefinders, one atop her forward superstructure and one each in her main gun turrets, and another 10 m unit atop her rear superstructure. Each 15.5 cm gun turret was equipped with an 8 m rangefinder. Low angle fire was controlled by two Type 98 fire control directors mounted above the rangefinders on the superstructure. Type 94 high-angle directors controlled the 12.7 mm AA guns, with Type 95 short-range directors for the 25 mm AA guns.

Musashi was built with a Type 0 hydrophone system in her bow. It was only usable while stationary or at low speed. In September 1942 a Type 21 air search radar was installed on the roof of the 15 m rangefinder at the top of the forward superstructure. Two Type 22 surface search radars were installed on the forward superstructure in July 1943. During repairs in April 1944, the Type 21 radar was replaced by a more modern one and a Type 13 early warning radar was fitted.

Aircraft

Musashi was designed to carry Mitsubishi F1M biplanes and Aichi E13A1 monoplanes. They were launched into the air by two 19.5 m long catapults, and a 6 tons crane, with 20 m long arm, was used to lift them out of the water. A system of trucks and trails, over the aft bridge, was used to move the floatplanes from the hangar to the catapults.

Launching

Musashi's keel was laid down on 29 March 1938 at Mitsubishi's Nagasaki shipyard, and was designated "Battleship No. 2". Throughout construction, a large curtain made of hemp rope weighing 408 tons prevented outsiders from viewing construction.

She was launched on 1 November 1940 in a secret ceremony attended only by a few top naval officials. The entry of such a large mass of steel into the water caused a light tsunami which propagated throughout the harbour up to local rives, flooding homes and capsizing small fishing boats.

Musashi was fitted out at nearby Sasebo, with Captain Kaoru Arima assigned as her commanding officer.

Service

The battleship *Musashi* was commissioned at Nagasaki on 5 August 1942 and assigned to the 1st Battleship Division together with *Yamato*, *Nagato* and *Mutsu*. Her secondary armament of 127 mm guns, 12 triple 25 mm gun mounts and four 13.2 mm anti-aircraft guns was fitted from 3 to 28 September 1942, as well as a Type 21 radar. The ship was working up for the rest of the year.

Musashi was assigned to the Combined Fleet, commanded by Admiral Isoroku Yamamoto, on 15 January 1943. Then, three days later, she moved to Truk, the main base in the South Pacific.

She officially became Yamamoto's flagship on 11 February, replacing her sister ship Yamato.

On 3 April, Admiral *Yamamoto* left *Musashi* and flew to Rabaul in New Britain to direct "Operation I-Go", a Japanese aerial offensive in the Solomon Islands. But his order were intercepted and his aircraft was shot down by American fighters. He was cremated and, on 23 April, his ashes were placed in his cabin onboard *Musashi* battleship.

On 17 May 1943 *Musashi*, in response to the American's operations in the Aleutian Islands, arrived at Yokosuka. But no contact was made with the American forces and the ships moved to Kure on 23 May, where Yamamoto's ashes were brought home, in preparation for a formal state funeral. On 9 June, Captain Keizo Komura was given command of the ship.

On 23 June 1943, on an inspection, *Musashi* was visited by Emperor Hirohito and his staff.

From 1 to 8 July 1943, at Kure, four Type 22 fire control radars were installed on the bridge.

From 5 August 1943 to 10 February 1944 *Musashi* had no significant activities, remaining mostly in port at Truk. In this period she only moved, leading a large fleet, in response to suspicions of planned American raids

on Wake Islands. But she failed to make contact with the Americans and returned to Truk on 26 October.

On 7 December 1943, Captain Bunji Asakura assumed command of *Musashi*, while Captain Komura was promoted to Rear Admiral and transferred to the Third Fleet.

From 15 and 24 February 1944, *Musashi* was used to transport one Imperial Japanese Army battalion, a Special Naval Landing Force battalion, munitions, fuel and vehicles from Yokosuka to the Palau Islands. She arrived at Palau on 29 February after losing most of the deck load of munitions during a typhoon. She departed Palau Islands on 29 March 1994, at night, but she was discovered by an American submarine. The submarine fired six torpedoes, but only one hit the battleship. The torpedo made a hole near the bow of *Musashi*, flooding her with 3000 tons of water. The hit killed seven crewmen and wounded another eleven. The battleship continued to sail for Japan at a reduced speed and reached Krune Naval Arsenal on 3 April. She was repaired and her anti-aircraft armament was enhanced. Six of her large 155 mm secondary guns were replaced with a large number of 25 mm anti-aircraft guns. She also was fitted with new radars, but still primitive compared to the American ones.

In May 1944 Captain Asakura was promoted to Rear Admiral. On 10 May, *Musashi* moved to Okinawa and on 12 May to Tawitawi where she and her sister Yamato were assigned to the 1st Mobile Fleet under the command of Vice Admiral Jisaburo Ozawa. On 10 June they moved to Batjan under the command of Vice Admiral Marome Ugaki for the Operation Kon, a counterattack against the American invasion of Biak. Two days later, due to the American attack on Saipan, Ugaki ordered to move towards the Mariana Islands. On 16 June they reached Ozawa's main force and the battleships were assigned to the 2nd Fleet commanded by Vice Admiral Takeo Kurita.

On 12 August Captain Toshihira Inoguchi assumed command of *Musashi*. Inoguchi was promoted to Rear Admiral after the assignment, on 15 October. Three days later *Musashi* moved for Brunei Bay to join the main Japanese Fleet to prepare the counterattack, named Operation Sho-1, against the American landings at Leyte. The fleet moved into the Sibuyan Sea, west of Leyte in the Philippine Islands, to attack the American transports on the other side of the island.

On 24 October, at 08:10, the fleet was spotted by an aircraft from carrier USS Intrepid. Two hours later *Musashi* was attacked by a number of Curtiss SB2C Helldiver dive bombers coming from Intrepid. One bomb hit the root of turret No. 1. Then *Musashi* was hit starboard amidships by a torpedo launched by a Grumman TFB Avenger.

About an hour and a half later *Musashi* was again under attack by a number of Helldivers from Intrepid. A bomb penetrated the port side deck and exploded above one of the engine room. The port side inboard propeller shaft lost power and the speed dropped to 22 knots (41 km/h). Other three torpedoes hit *Musashi* on the port side causing serious damages. During the attack, *Musashi* fired anti-aircraft shells from her main guns, but one shell detonated in the middle of Turret No. 1 destroying it.

Another squadron of 29 aircrafts from carriers Essex and Lexington came to attack the battleship. She was hit by four more torpedoes causing extensive flooding. Two hours later nine Helldivers from Enterprise attacked the battleship. Three more torpedoes reached the target, opening up *Musashi*'s starboard bow.

At 15:25 other 37 aircraft from Intrepid, Franklin and Cabot reached *Musashi*. She was hit by a large number of bombs and by 11 torpedoes more. Her speed was reduced to 6 knots (11 km/h). In total *Musashi* was hit by 19 torpedoes and 17 bombs.

During the attack, five Avengers and five Helldivers were shot down. *Musashi* capsized at 19:36 and sank. Admiral Inoguchi did not abandon his ship and he went down with her. 1376 men, out of a total of 2399, were rescued.

General characteristics

Name	*Musashi*
Ordered	June 1937
Builder	Mitsubishi Shipyard, Nagasaki
Laid down	29 March 1938
Launched	1 November 1940
Commissioned	5 August 1942
Fate	Sunk, 24 October 1944
Class and type	Yamato class battleship
Displacement	68 200 long tons (69 300 t) normal 72 800 long tons (74 000 t) full load
Length	263 m (862 ft 10 in) overall
Beam	36.9 m (121 ft 1 in)
Draft	10.86 m (35ft 8 in) full load
Installed power	150 000 shp (110 000kW)
Propulsion	4 x propellers 4 x steam turbines
Speed	27.46 knots (50.86 km/h – 31.60 mph)
Range	7200 nmi (13 300 km–8300 mi) at 16 knots (30 km/h – 18 mph)
Crew	2500/2800 officers and men
Sensor and processing systems	1 x Type 21 air search radar 1 x Type 0 hydrophone system
Armament (October 1944)	3 triple 46 cm Type 94 guns 2 triple 15.5 cm 3rd Year Type guns 6 double 12.7 cm Type 89 35 triple, 25 single 25 mm Type 96 AA guns 2 twin 13.2 mm Type 93 AA Mgs
Armour	Waterline belt: 410 mm (16.1 in) Deck: 200–300 mm (7.9–9.1 in) Gun turrets: 250–650 mm (9.8–25.6 in) Barbettes: 380–560 mm (15–22 in) Conning tower: 500 mm (19.7 in) Bulkheads: 300–340 mm (11.8–13.4 in)
Aircraft carried	6–7 floatplanes Mitsubishi F1M biplanes and Aichi E13A1 monoplanes

Front view.

Back view.

Bibliography

The battleship Yamato – Janusz Skulski.

IJN Battleship Musashi, tabular record of movement by Bob Hackett and Sander Kingsepp.

Reports of Damage to Japanese Warships (U.S. Naval Technical Mission to Japan – January 1946).

View of ship's hull and superstructures from starboard side.

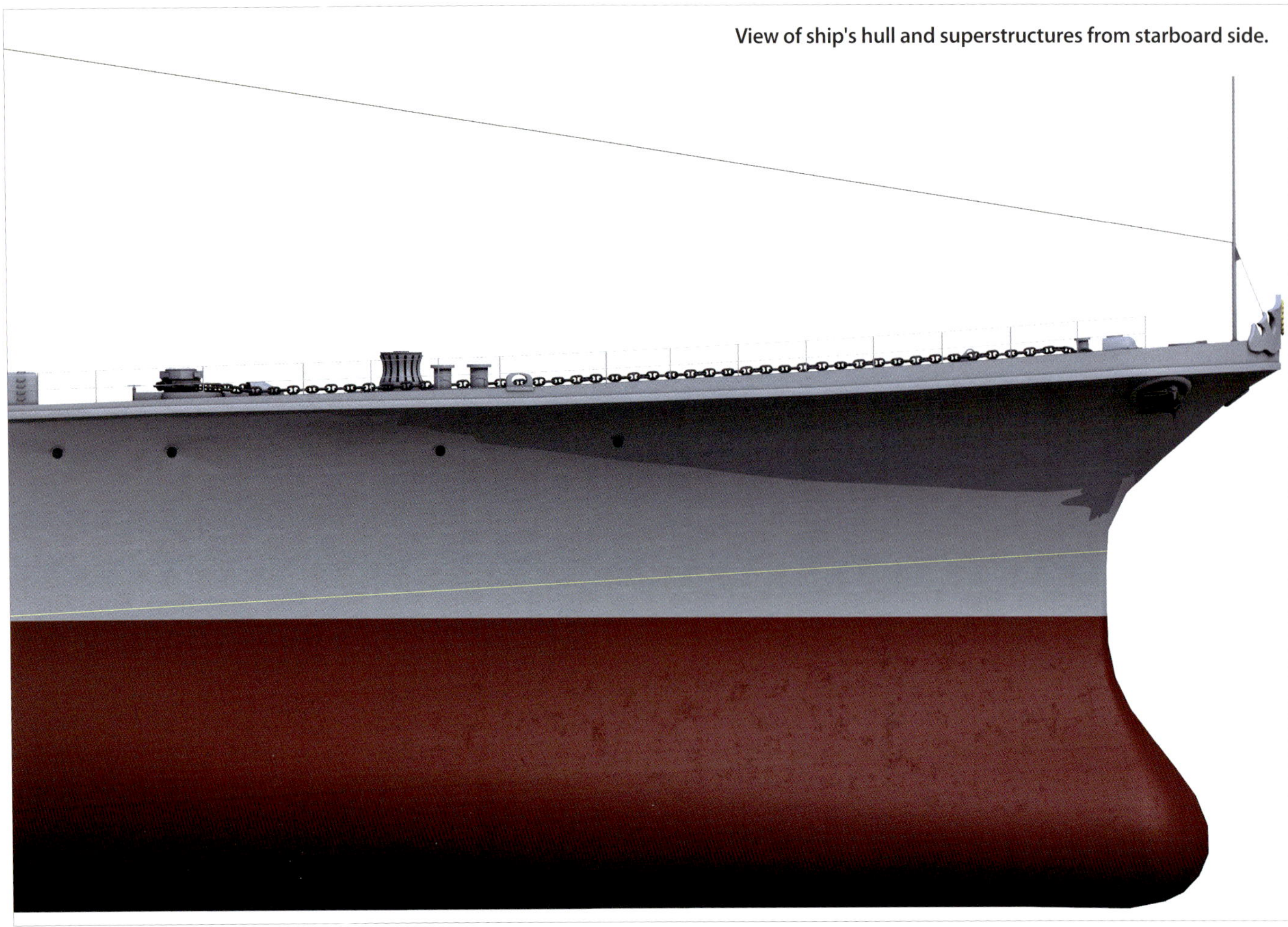

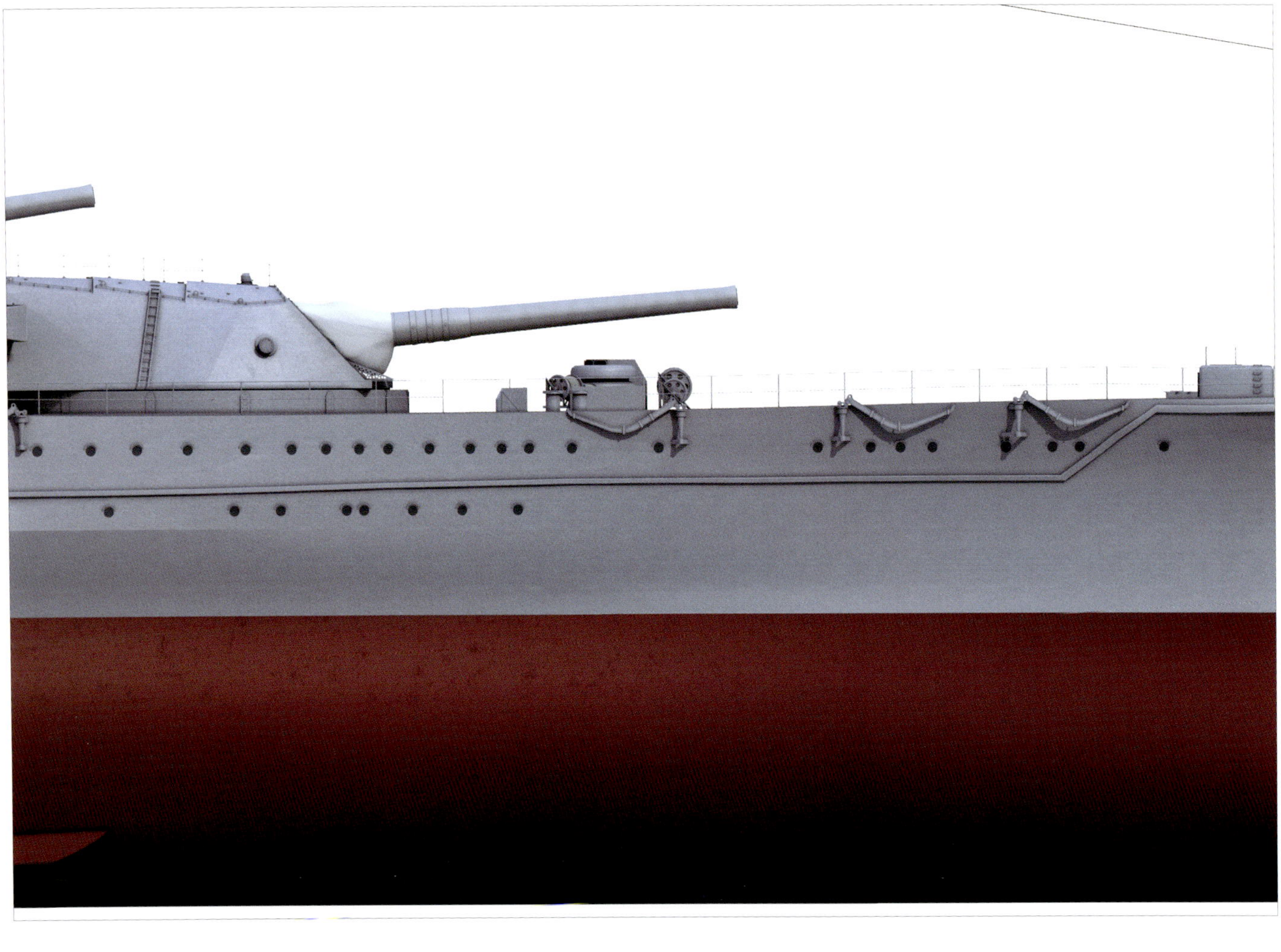

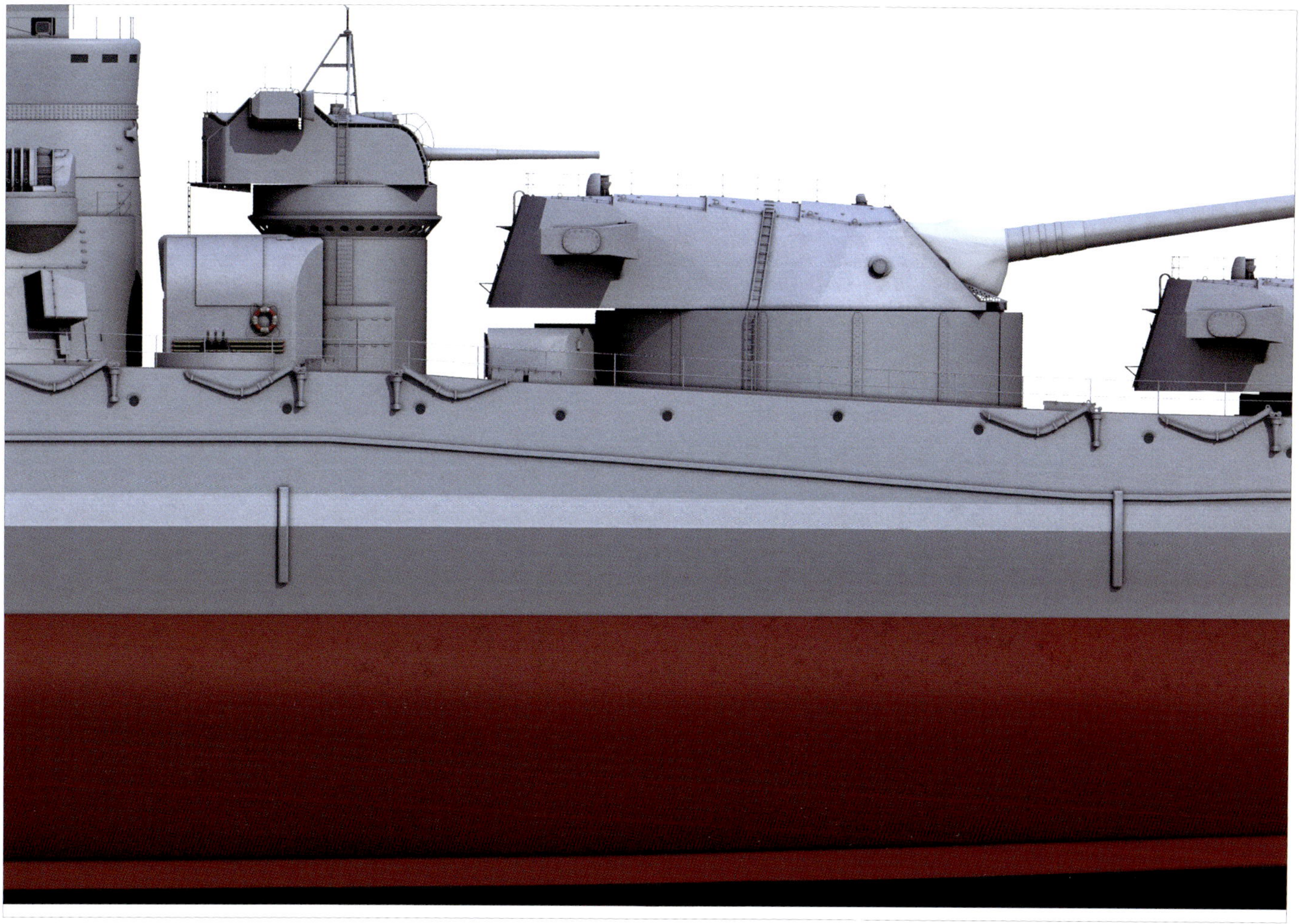

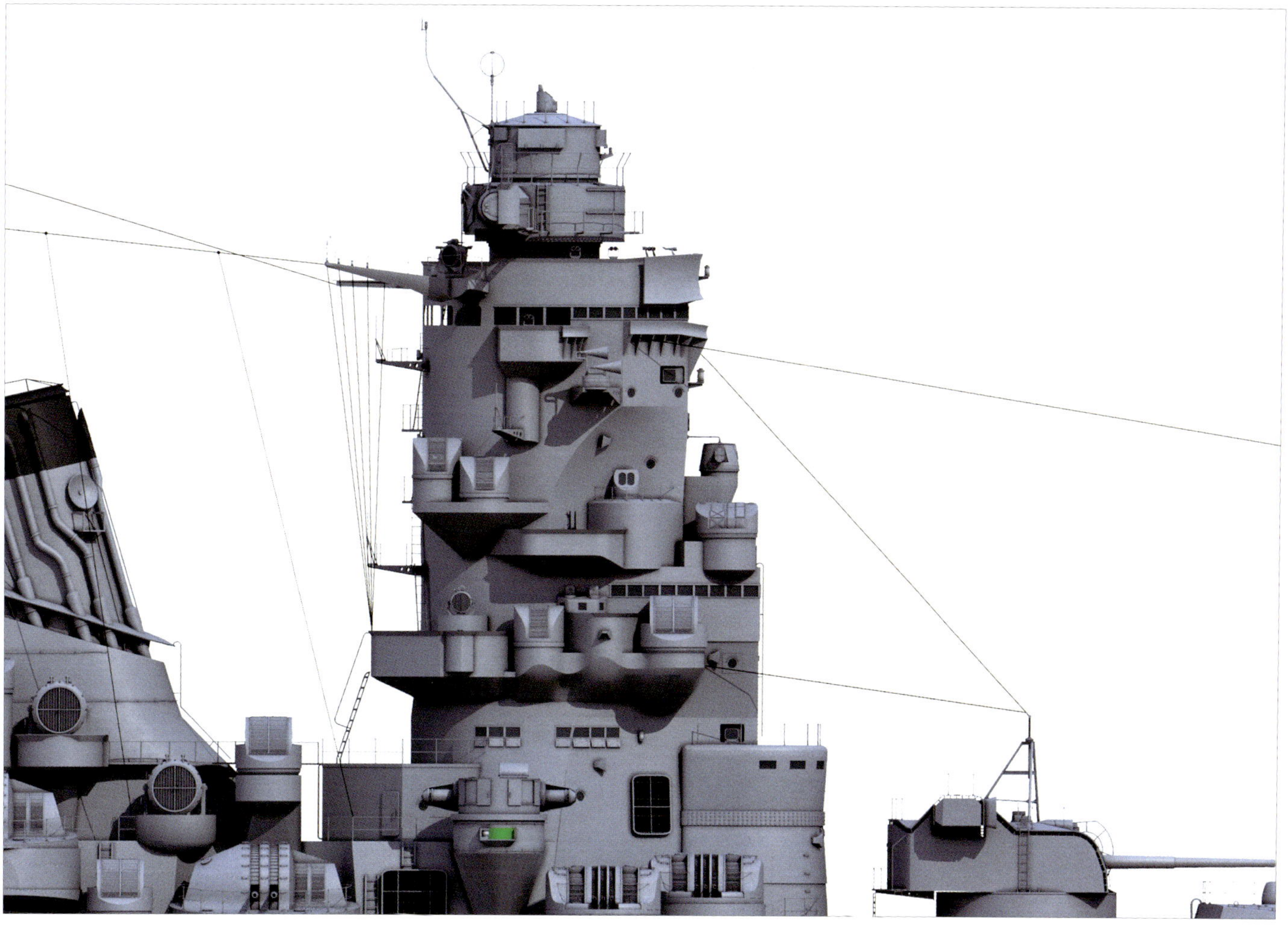

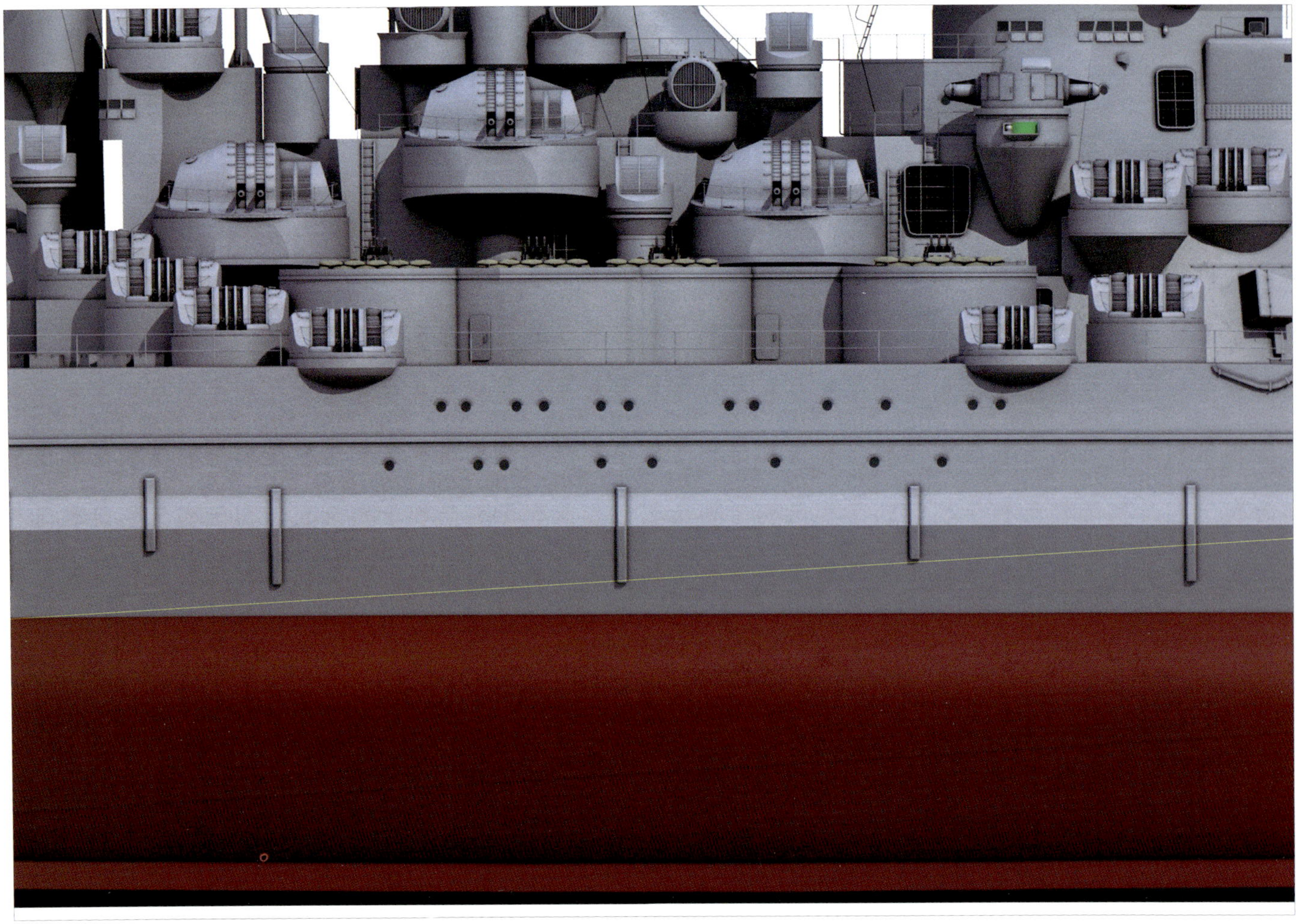

212-01

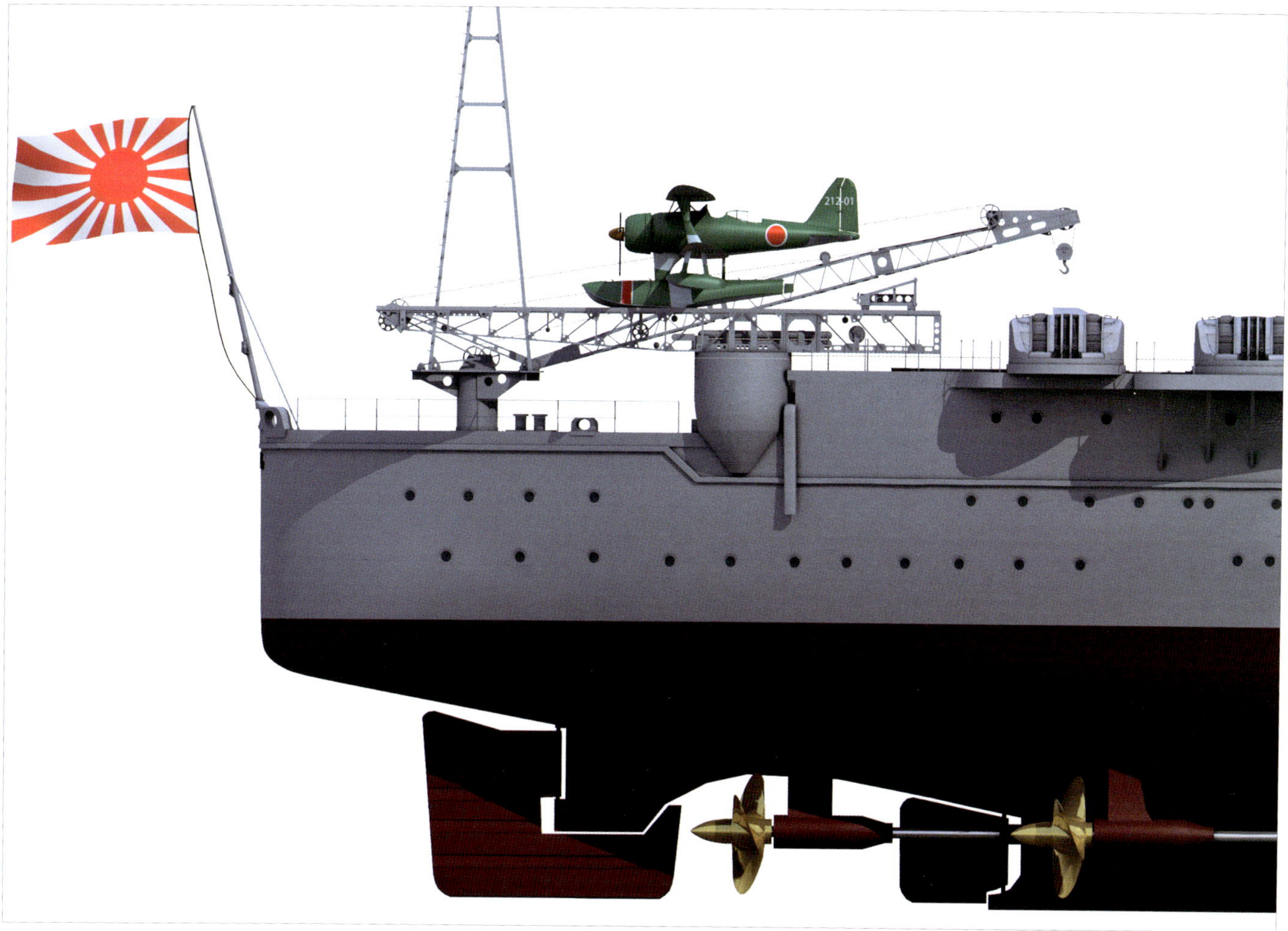
212-01

View of ship's hull and superstructures from port side.

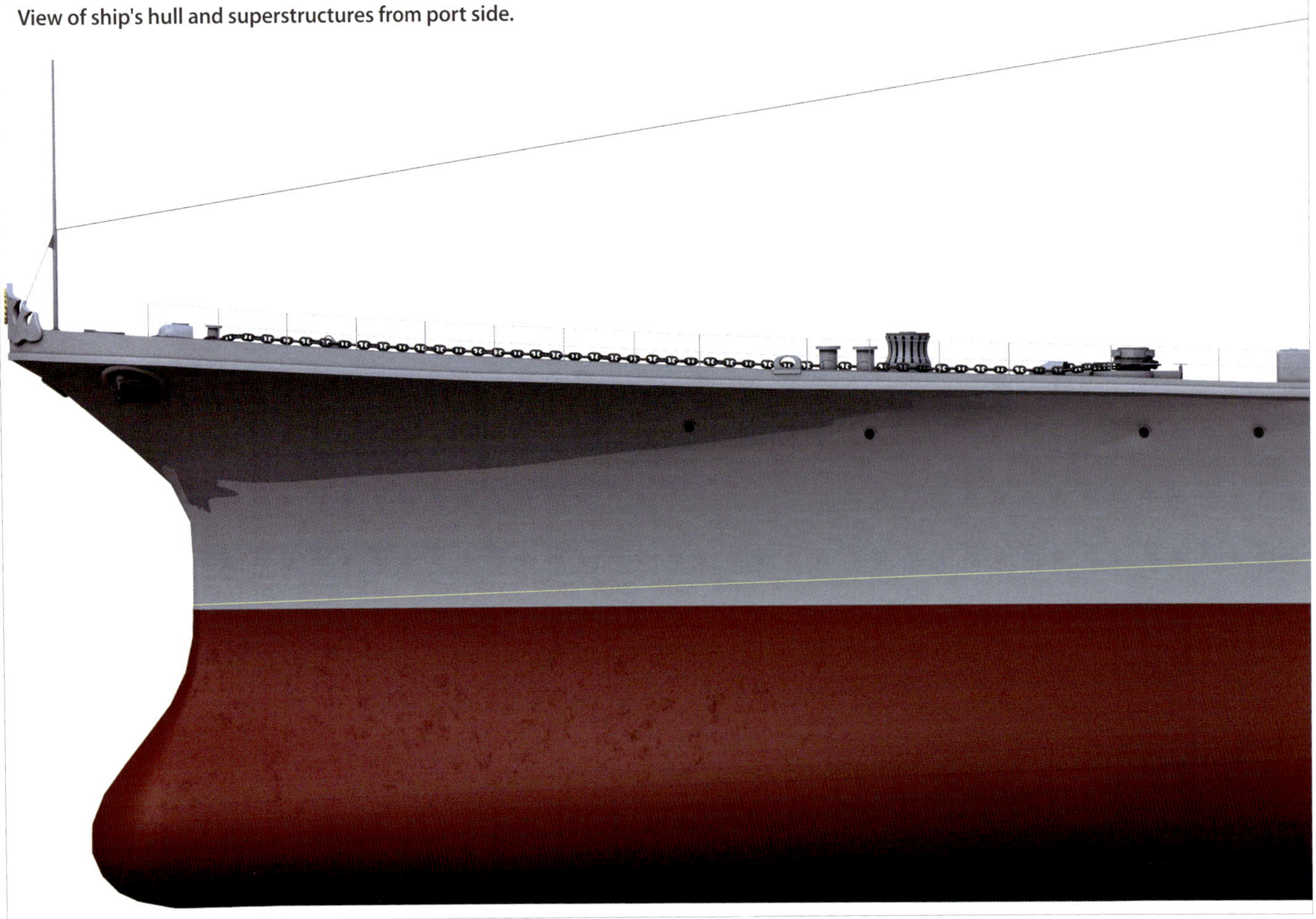

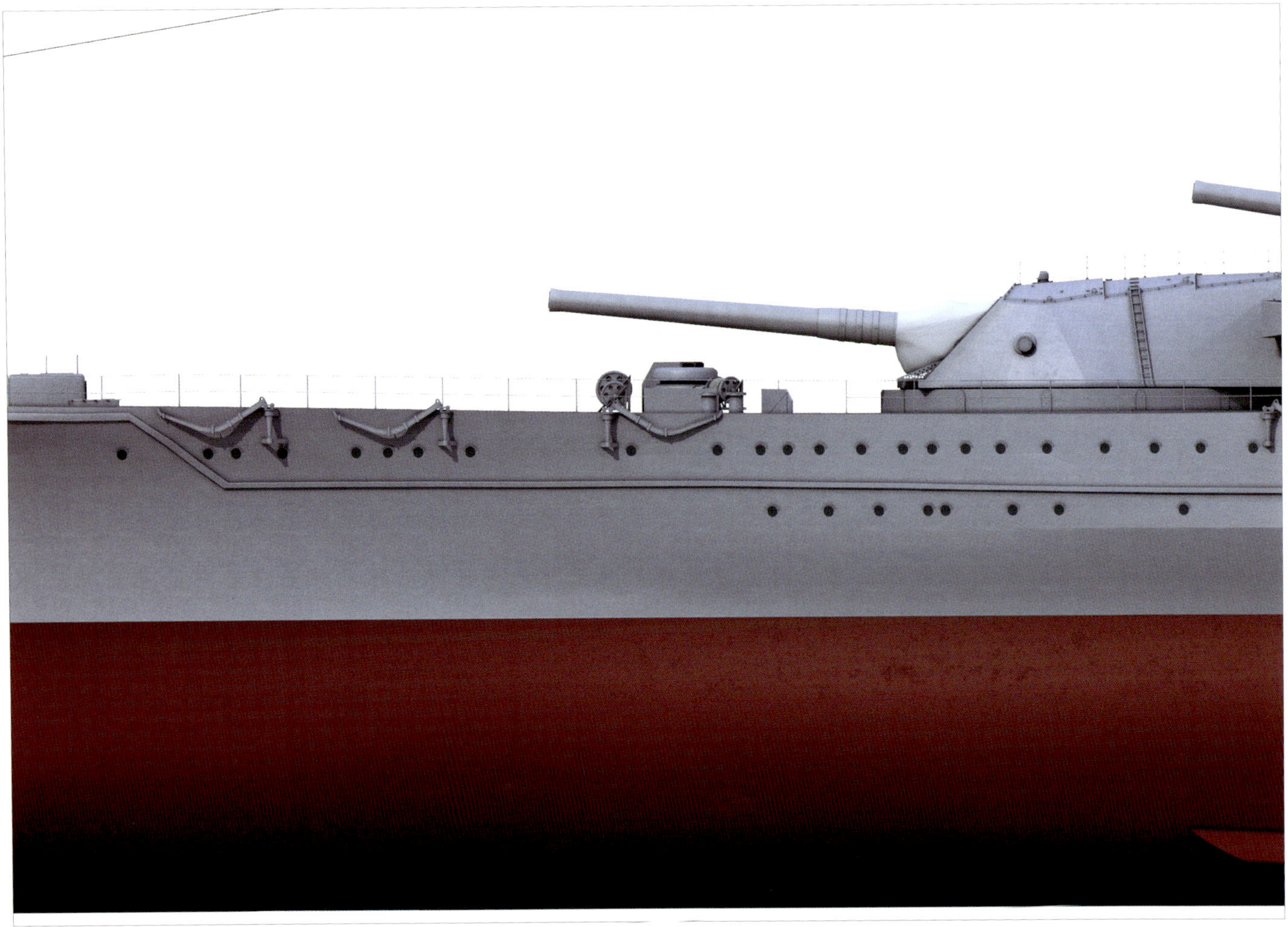

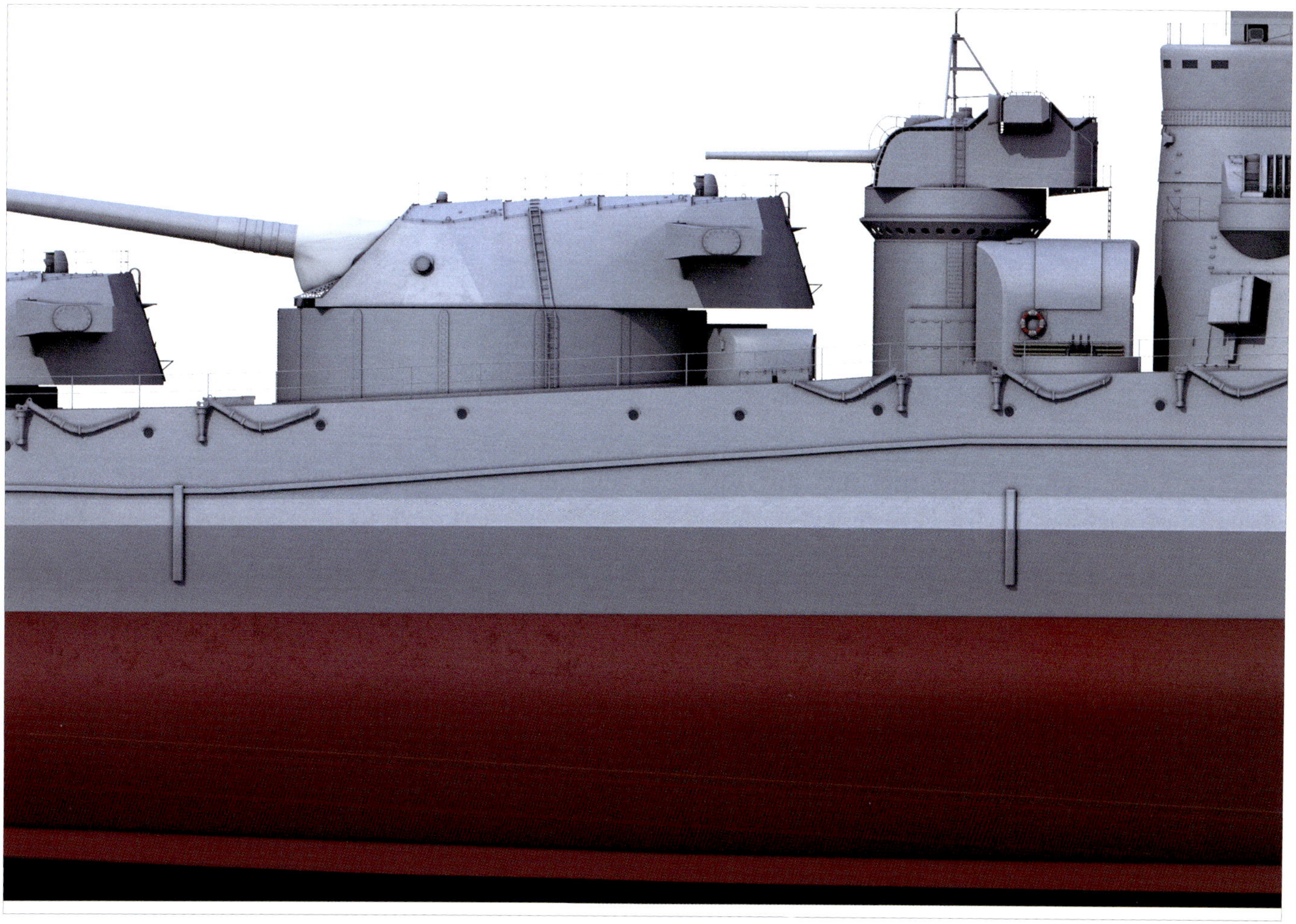

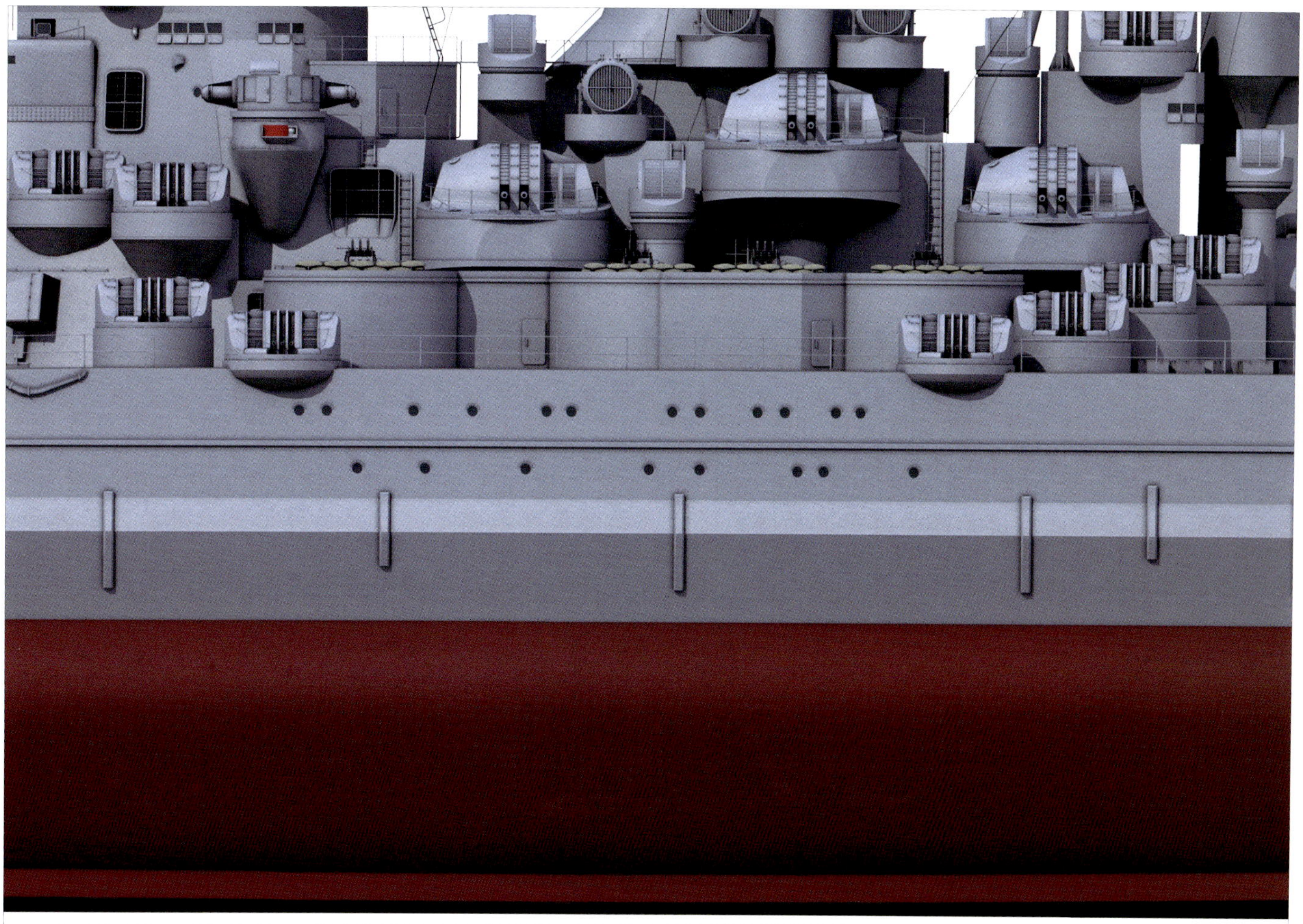

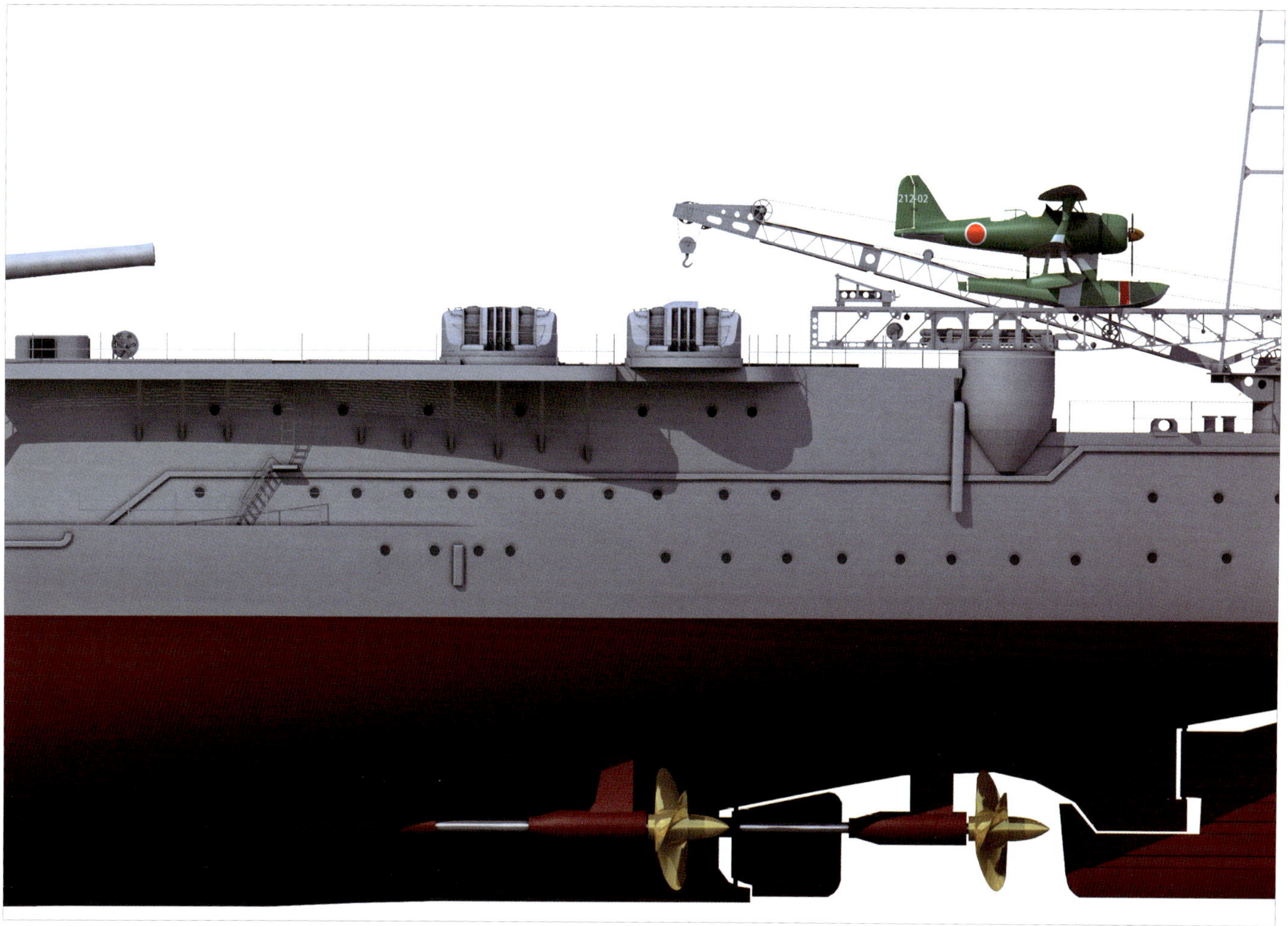
212-02

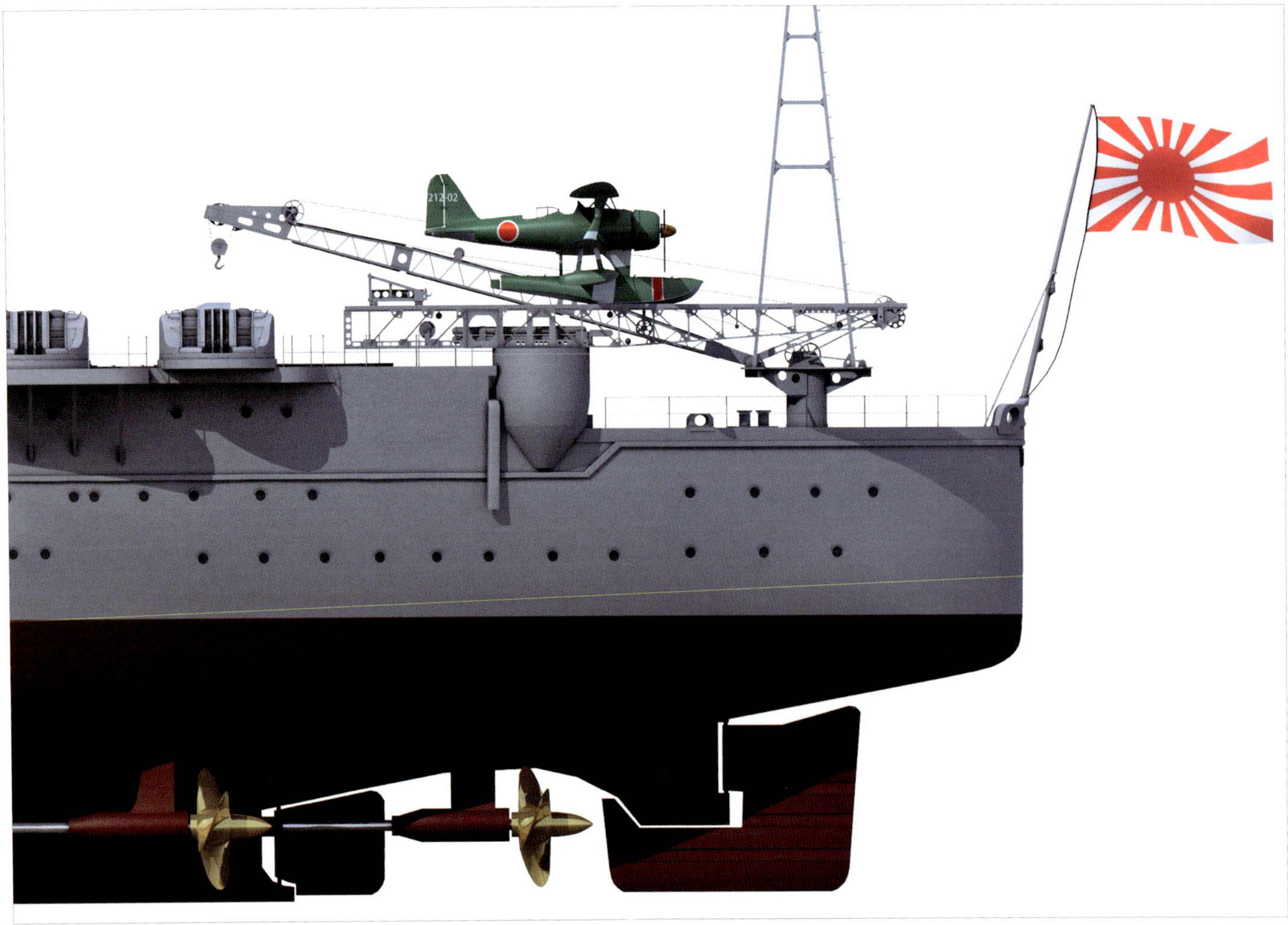

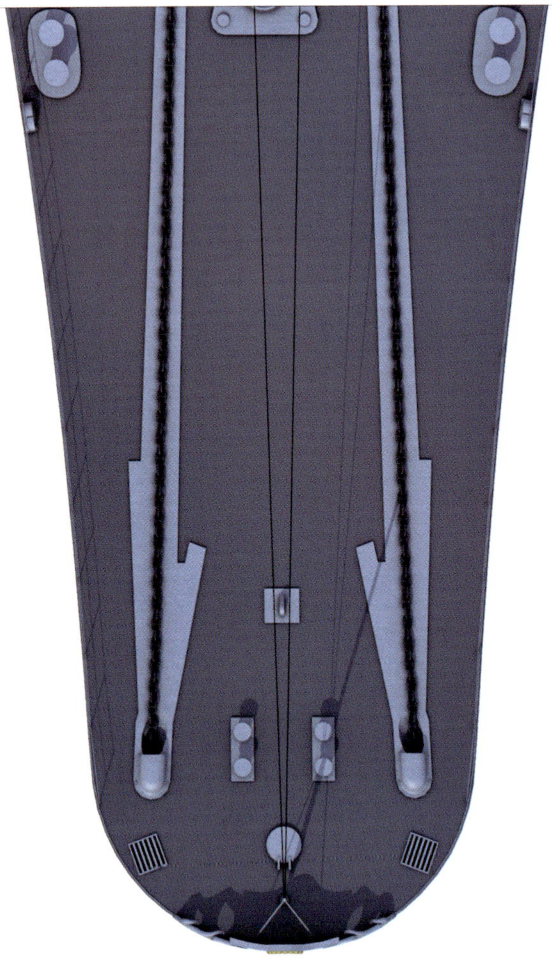

View of ship's hull and superstructures from top.

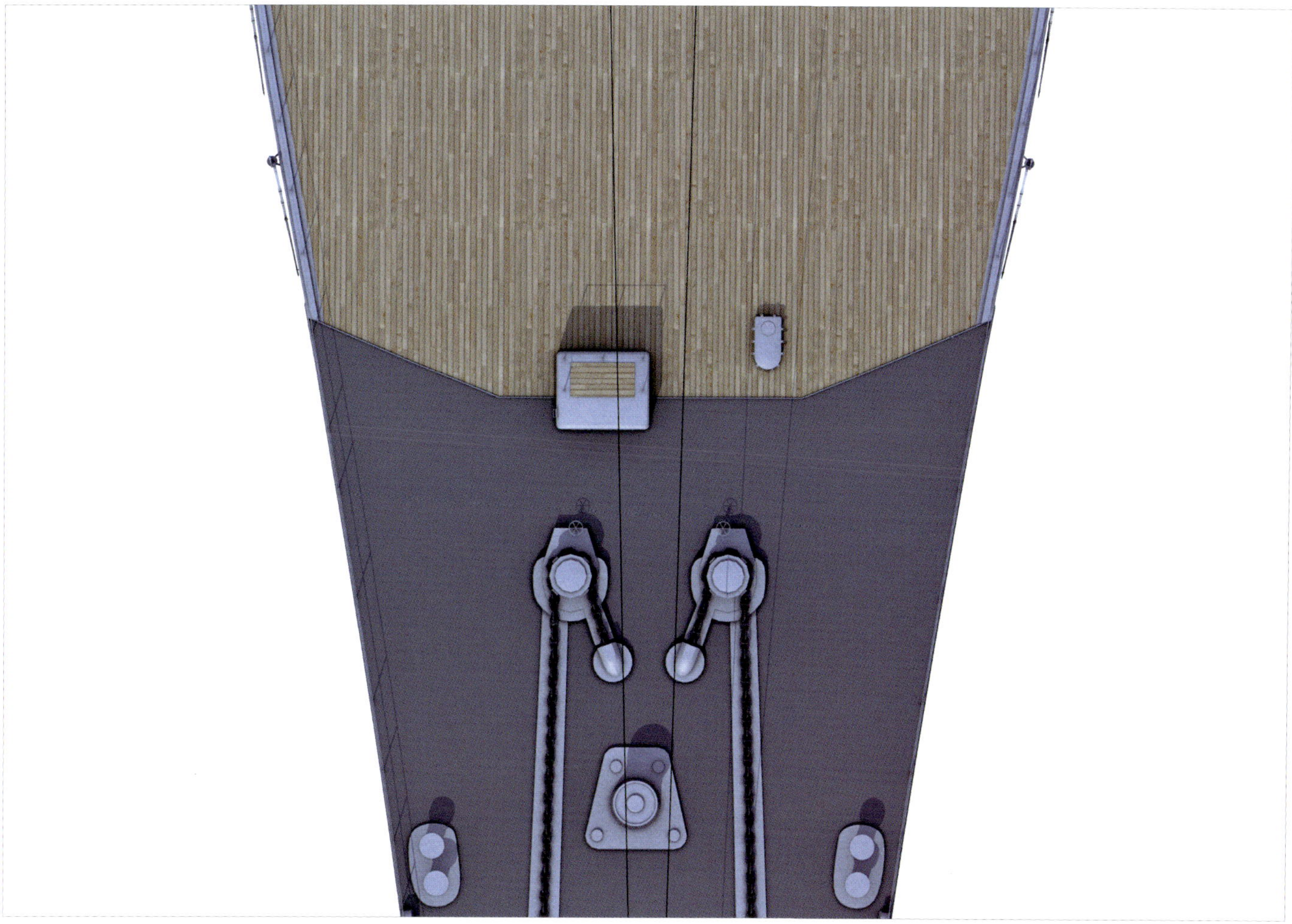

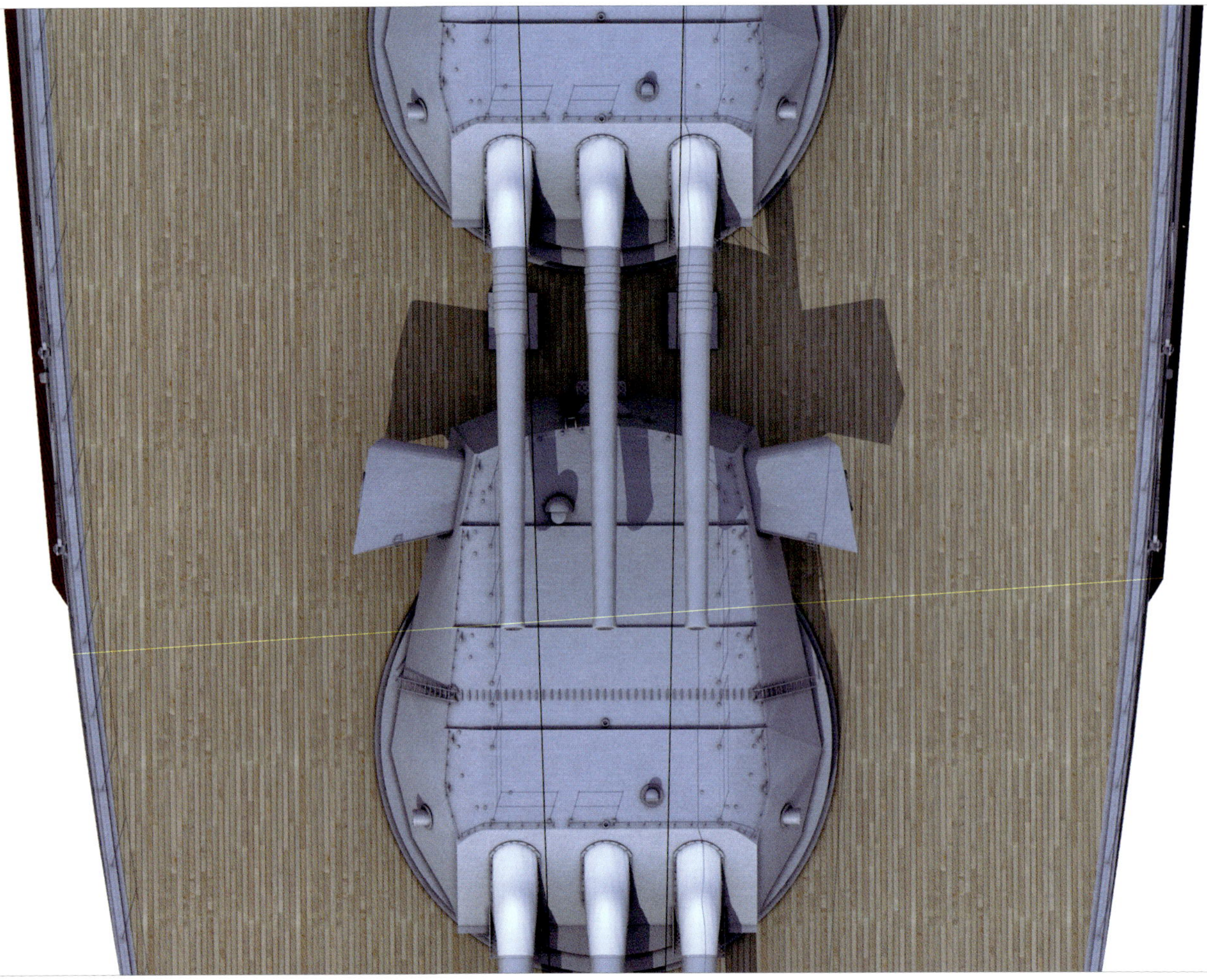

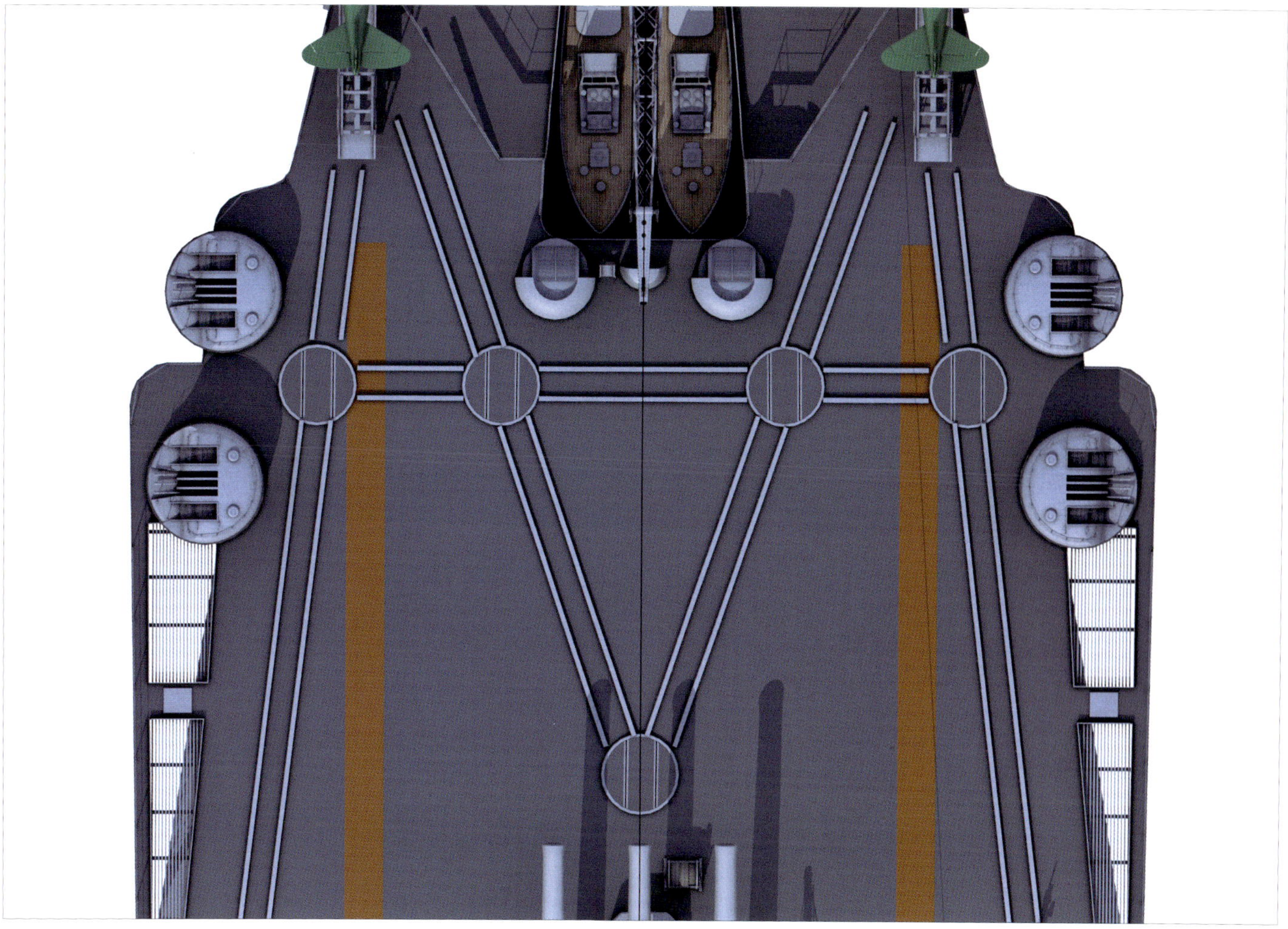

Overall view of the bow.

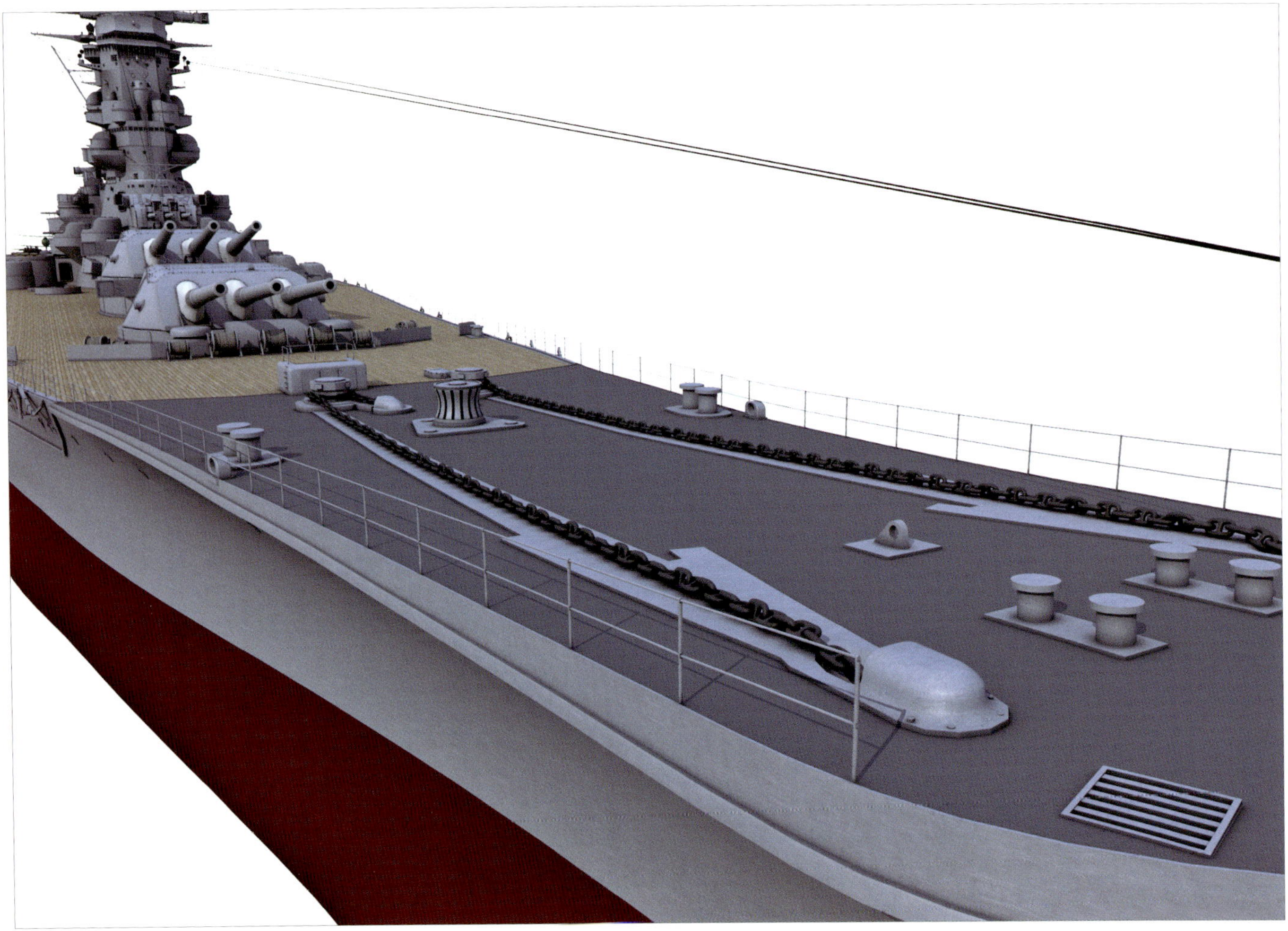

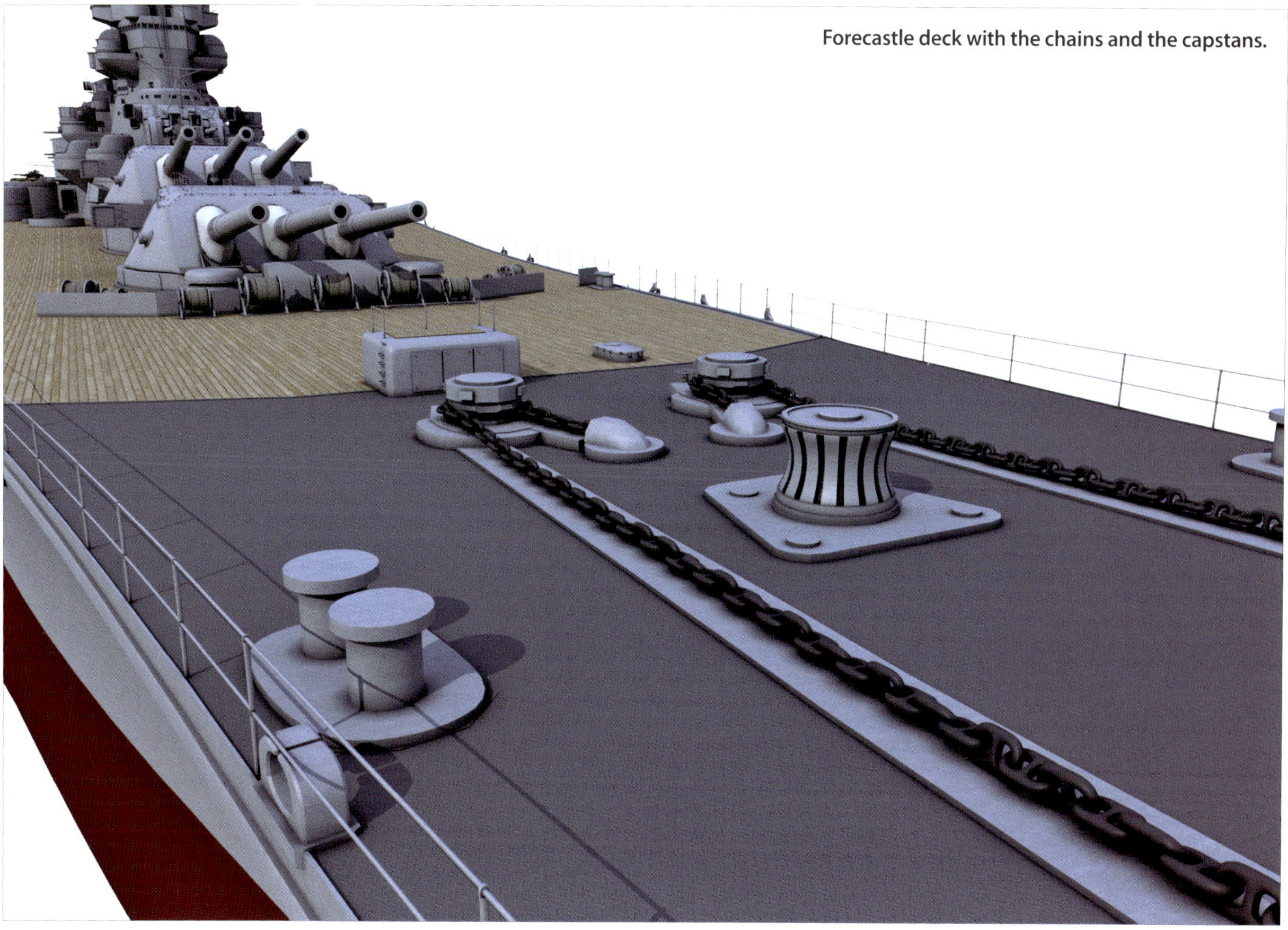

Forecastle deck with the chains and the capstans.

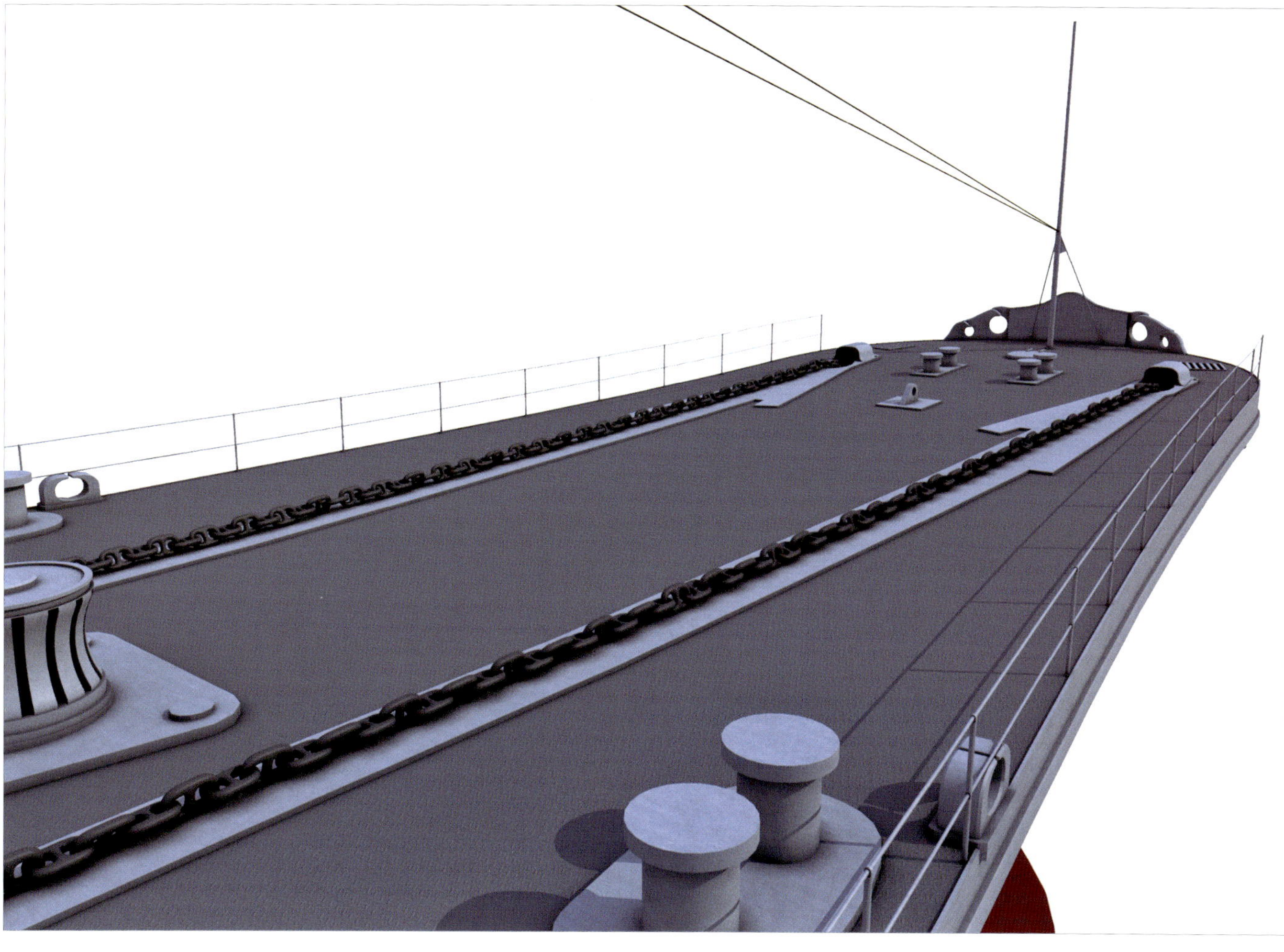

Overall view of the forecastle deck with the chains and the capstans from port side.

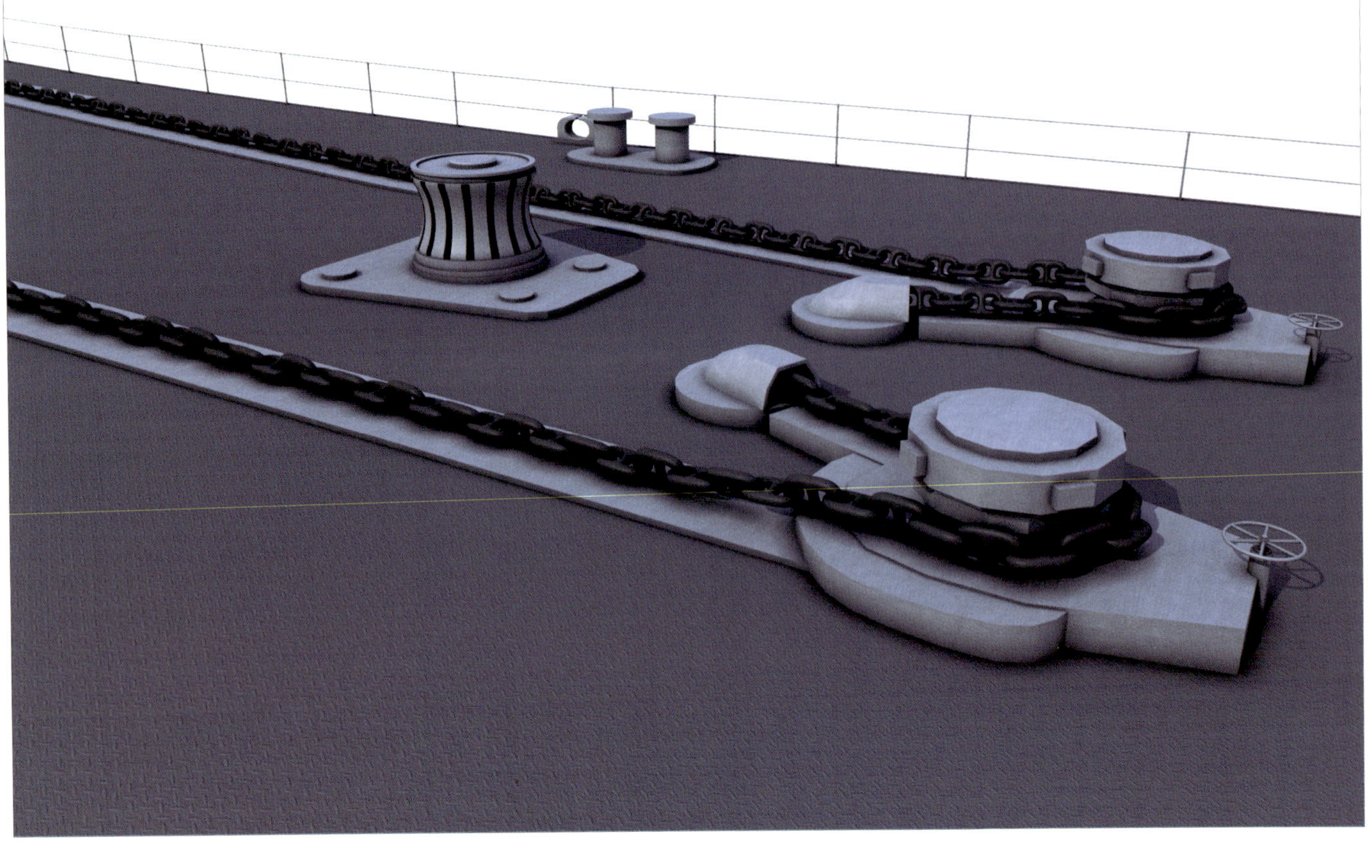

Overall view of the forecastle deck.

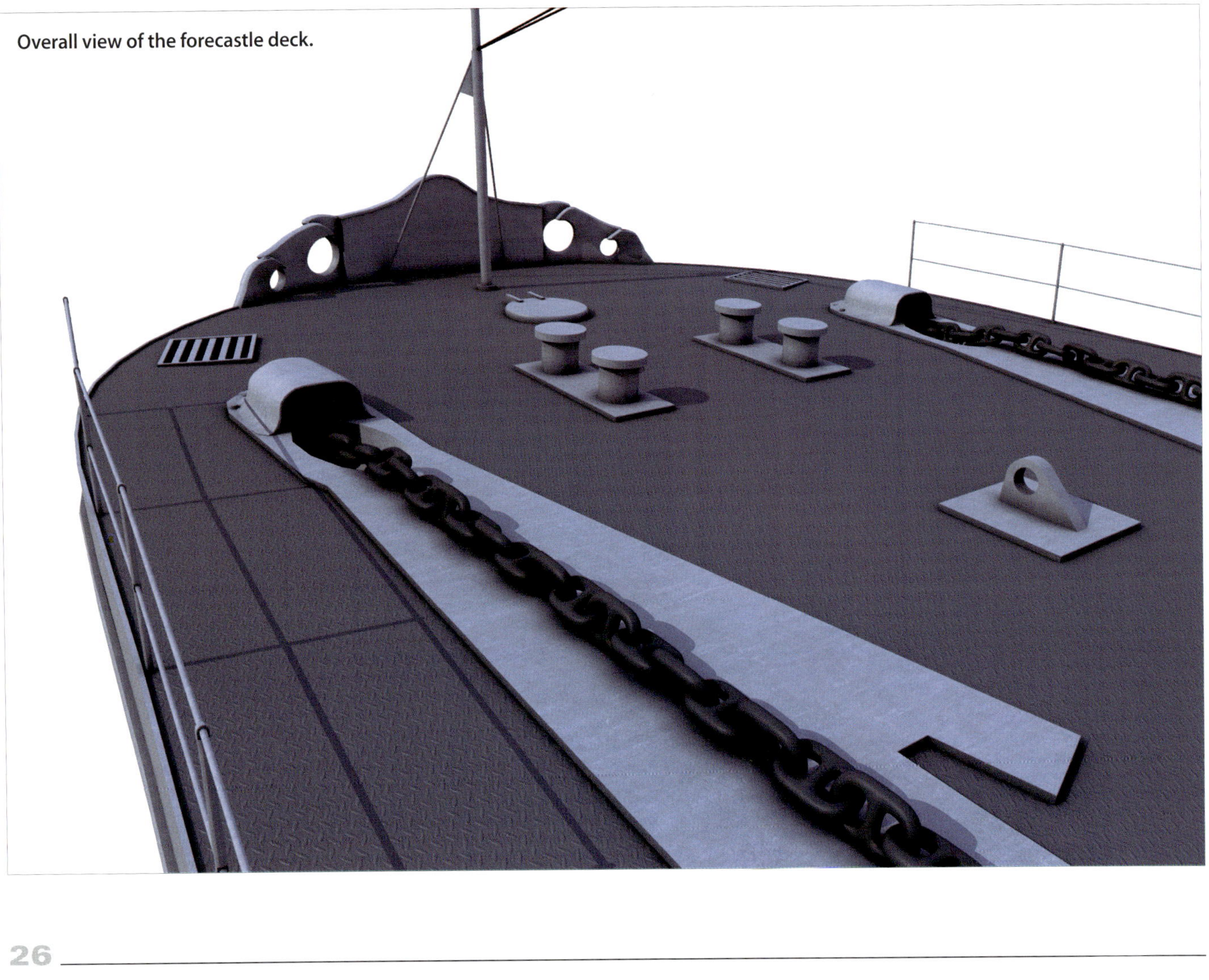

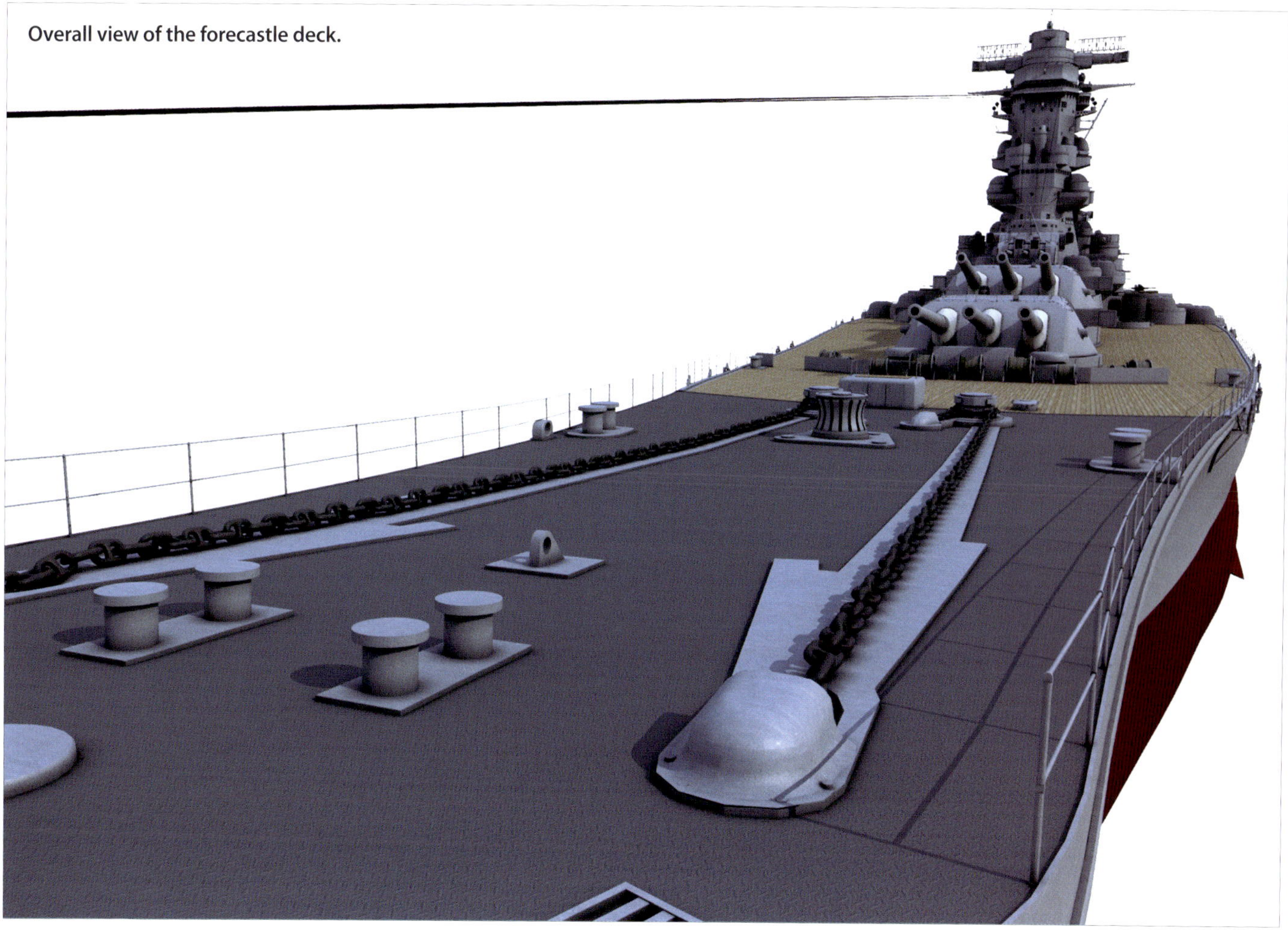

Overall view of the forecastle deck.

Overall view of the bow with the chrysanthemum crest.

Forecastle deck with the chains, the capstans and the small deck platform.

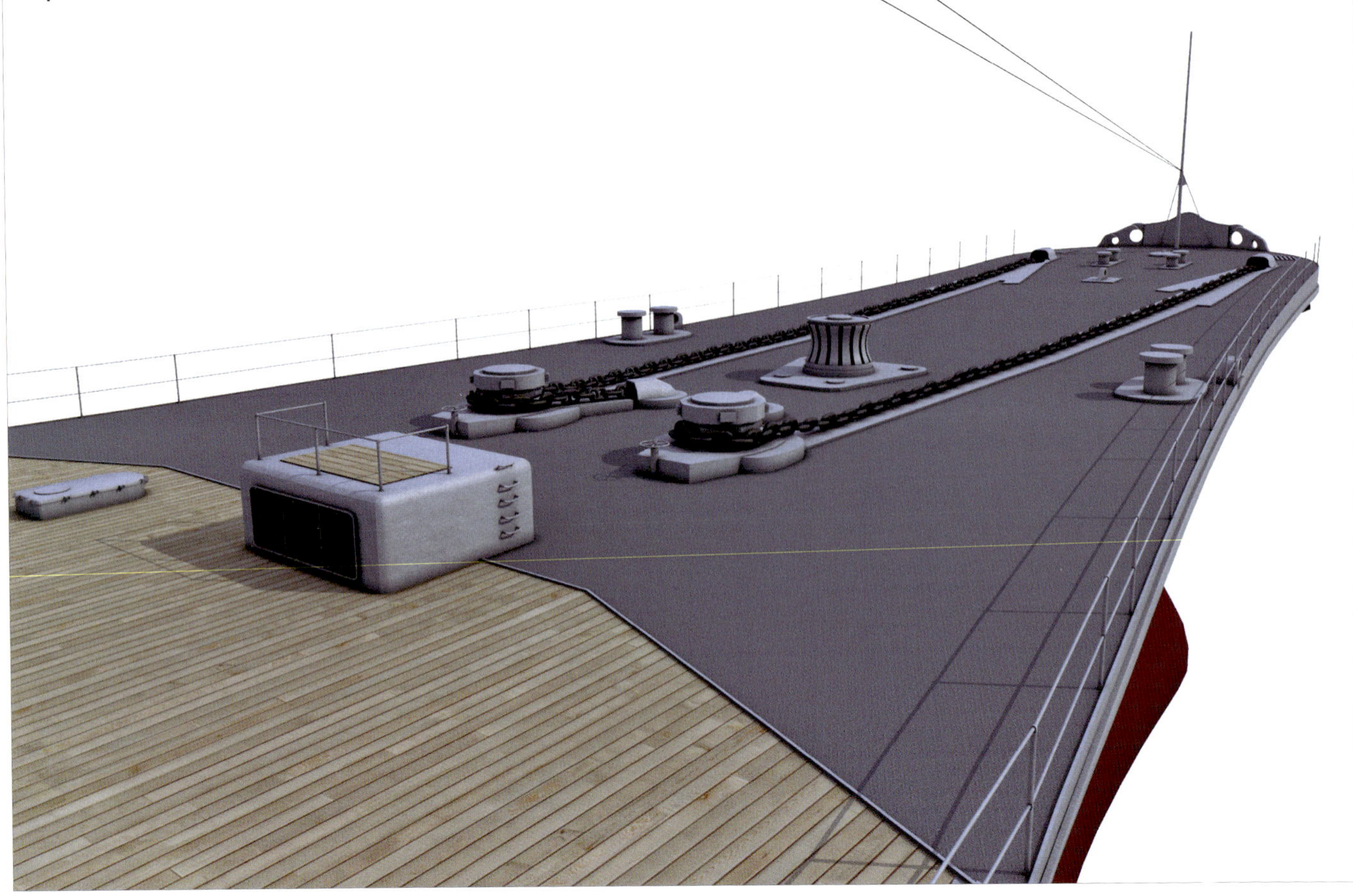

Forecastle deck with the ventilators and the small deck platform.

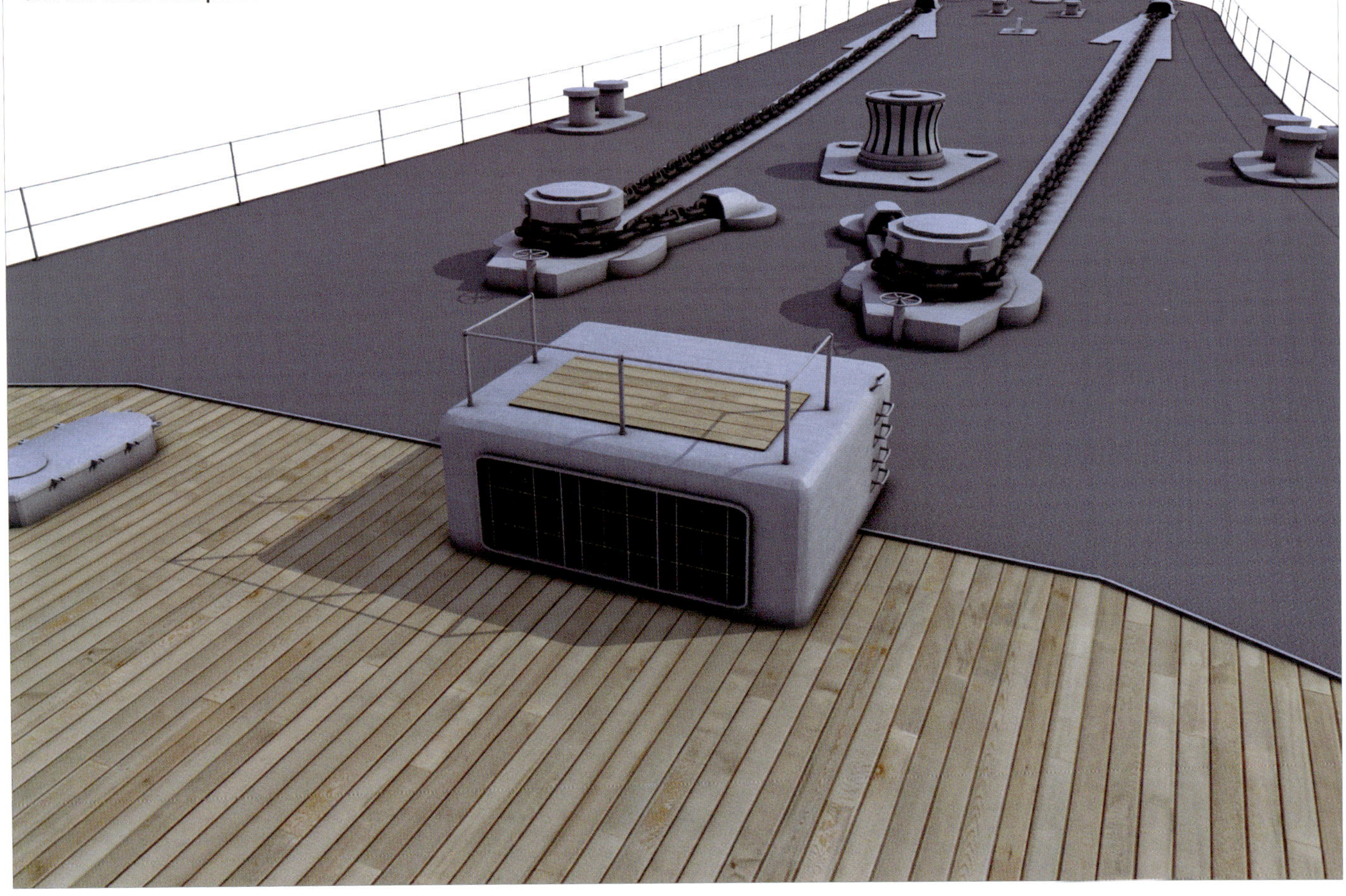

Overall view of the 46 cm turret No. 1.

Close view of the 46 cm turret No. 2 from port side.

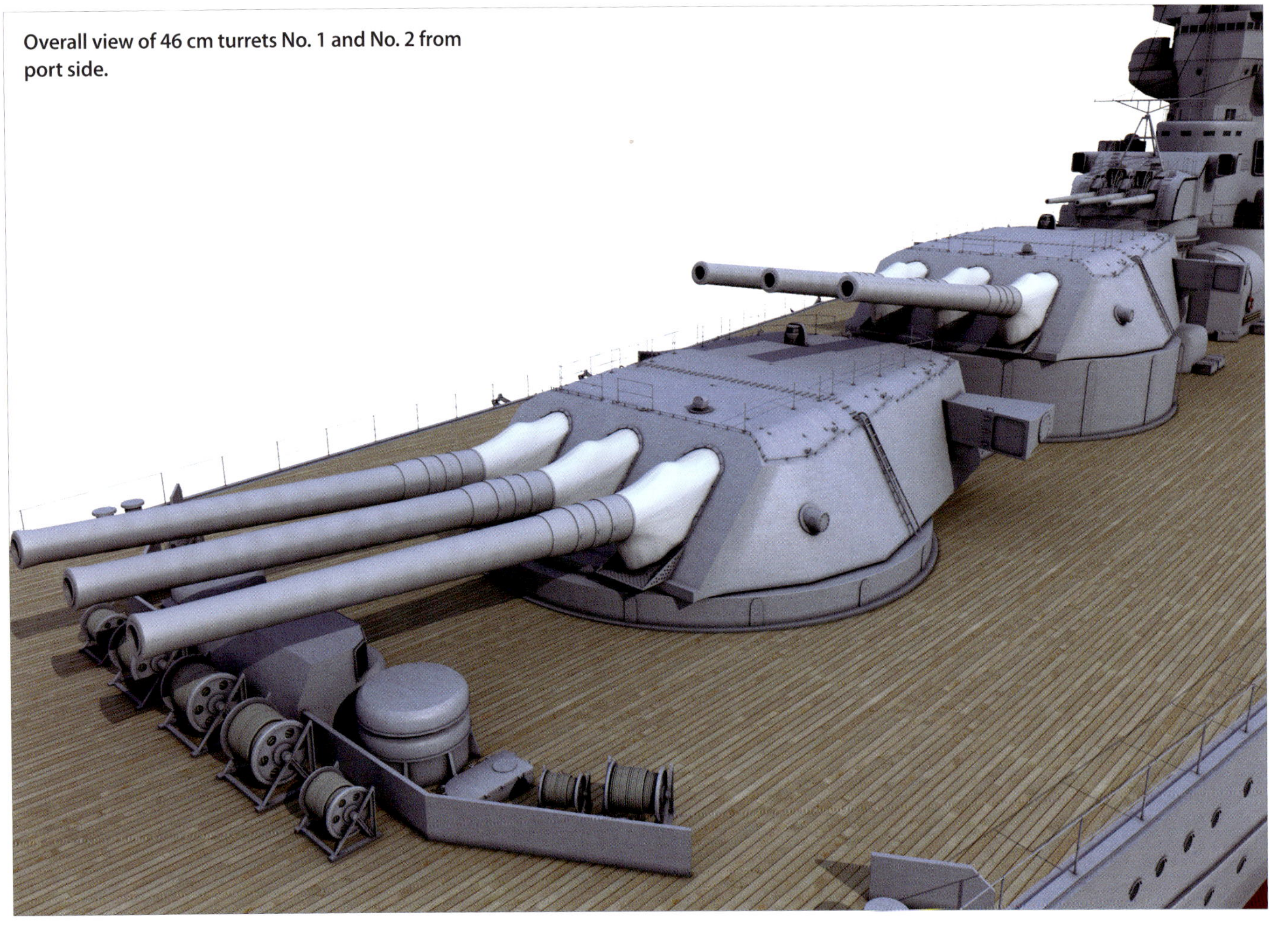

Overall view of 46 cm turrets No. 1 and No. 2 from port side.

Ventilators on the deck below the turret No. 1 guns.

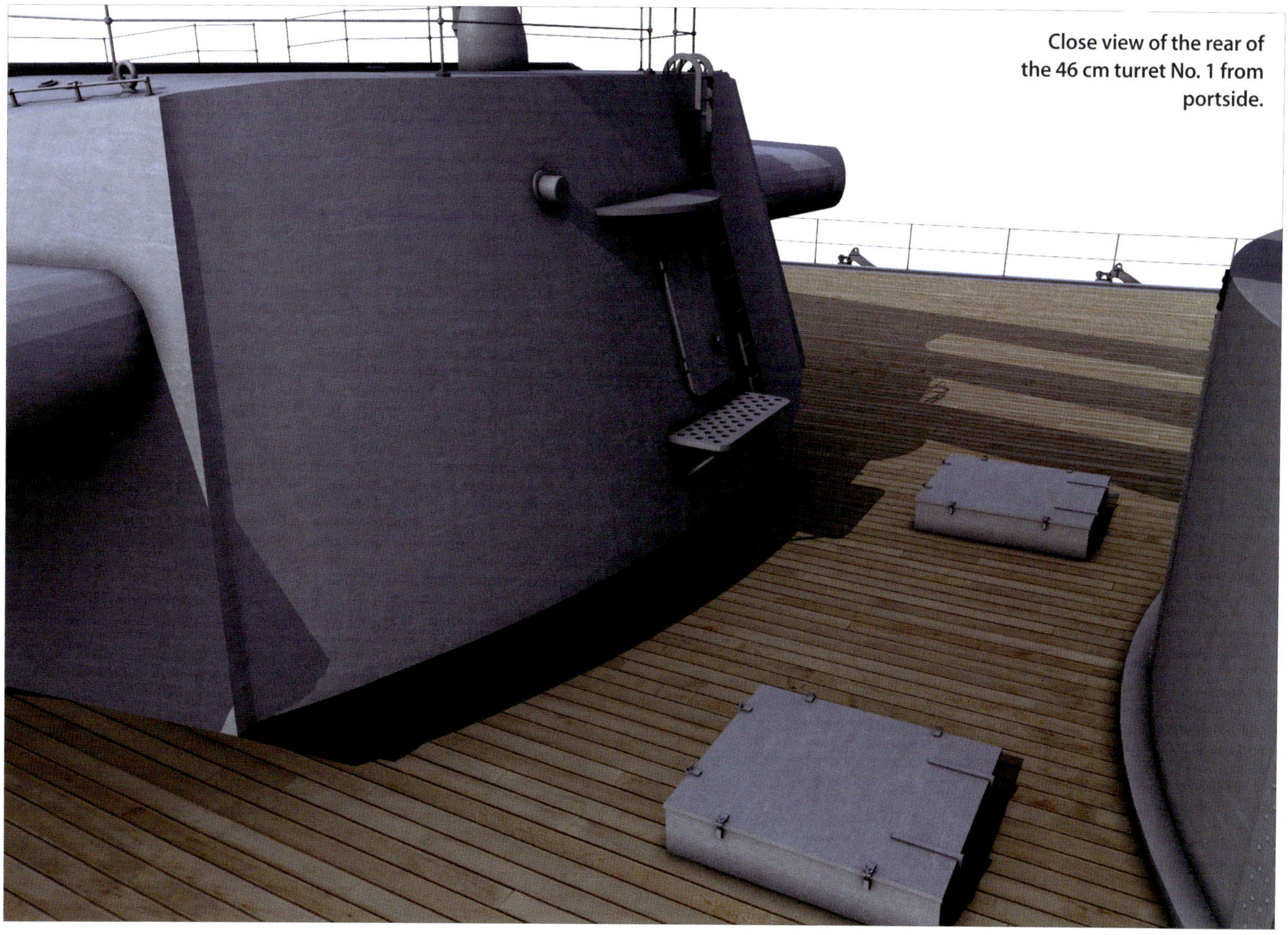
Close view of the rear of the 46 cm turret No. 1 from portside.

Top view of 46 cm turrets No. 1 and No. 2.

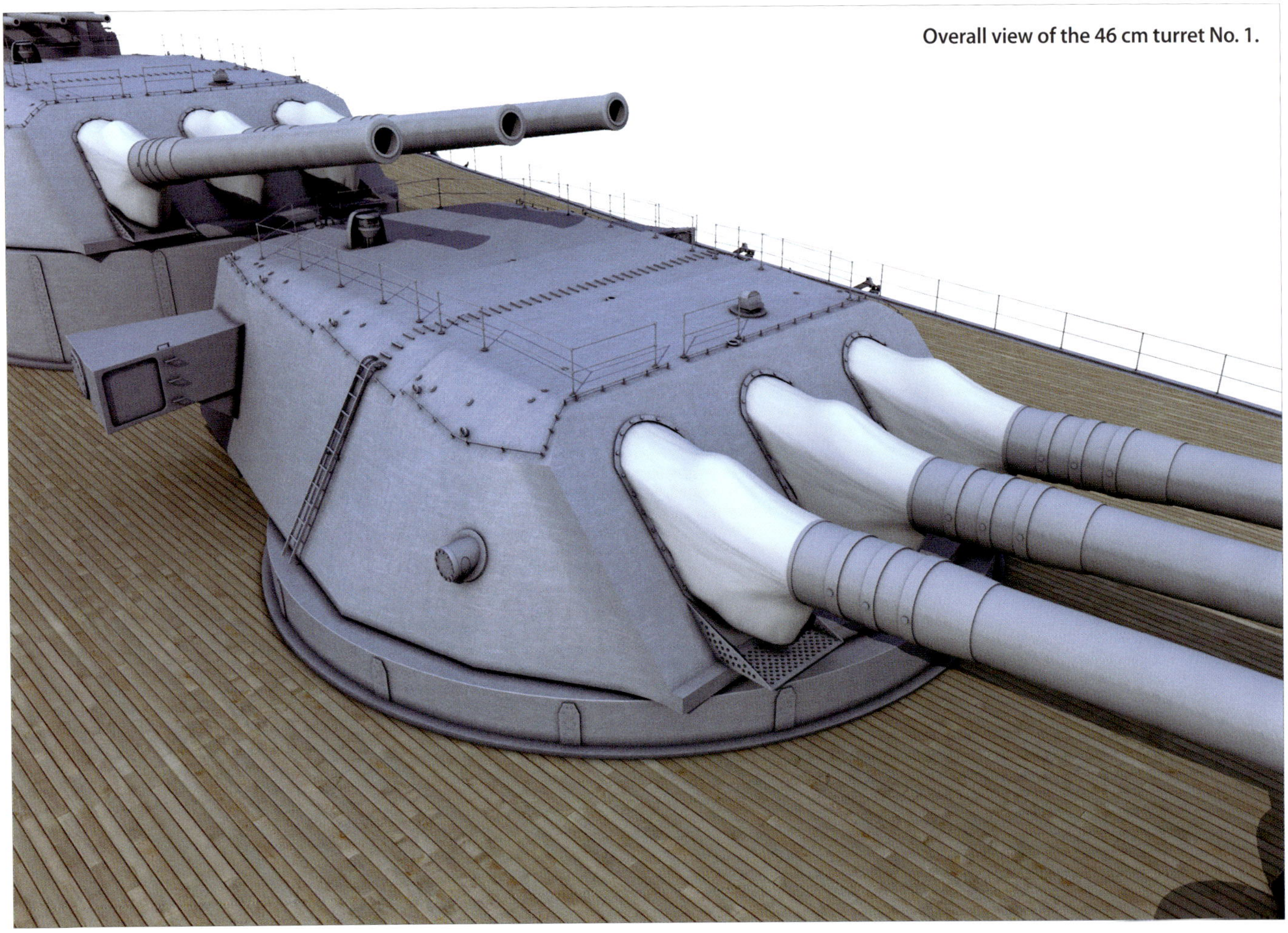
Overall view of the 46 cm turret No. 1.

Overall view of the 46 cm turret No. 2.

View ot the 46 cm turret No. 2.

Overall view of the forecastle deck with the two 46 cm turrets.

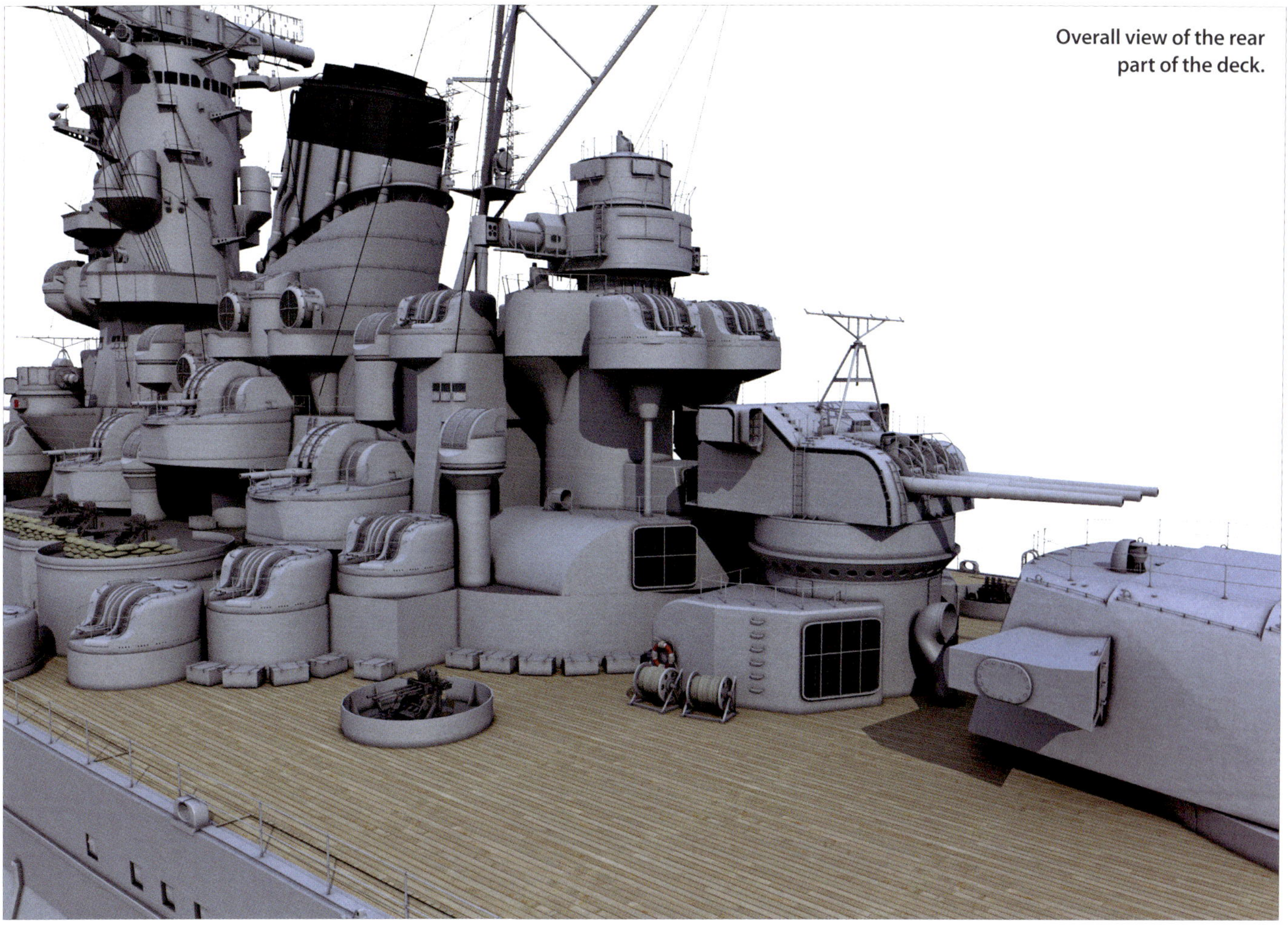

Overall view of the rear part of the deck.

Ventilators under the rear of the 46 cm turret No. 2.

Overall view of the 15.5 cm turret 'Nendo Shiki' No. 1.

View of the 15.5 cm turret 'Nendo Shiki' No. 1.

View of the 15.5 cm turret 'Nendo Shiki' No. 1.

▲ View of the basement of the 15.5 cm turret 'Nendo Shiki' No. 1.

▼ Overall view of the conning tower.

View of two Type 96 'Shiki' triple 25 mm AA gun from starboard side.

Close view of two Type 96 'Shiki' triple 25 mm AA gun from starboard side.

View of gun and searchlight control tower fitted at side of compass bridge starboard side.

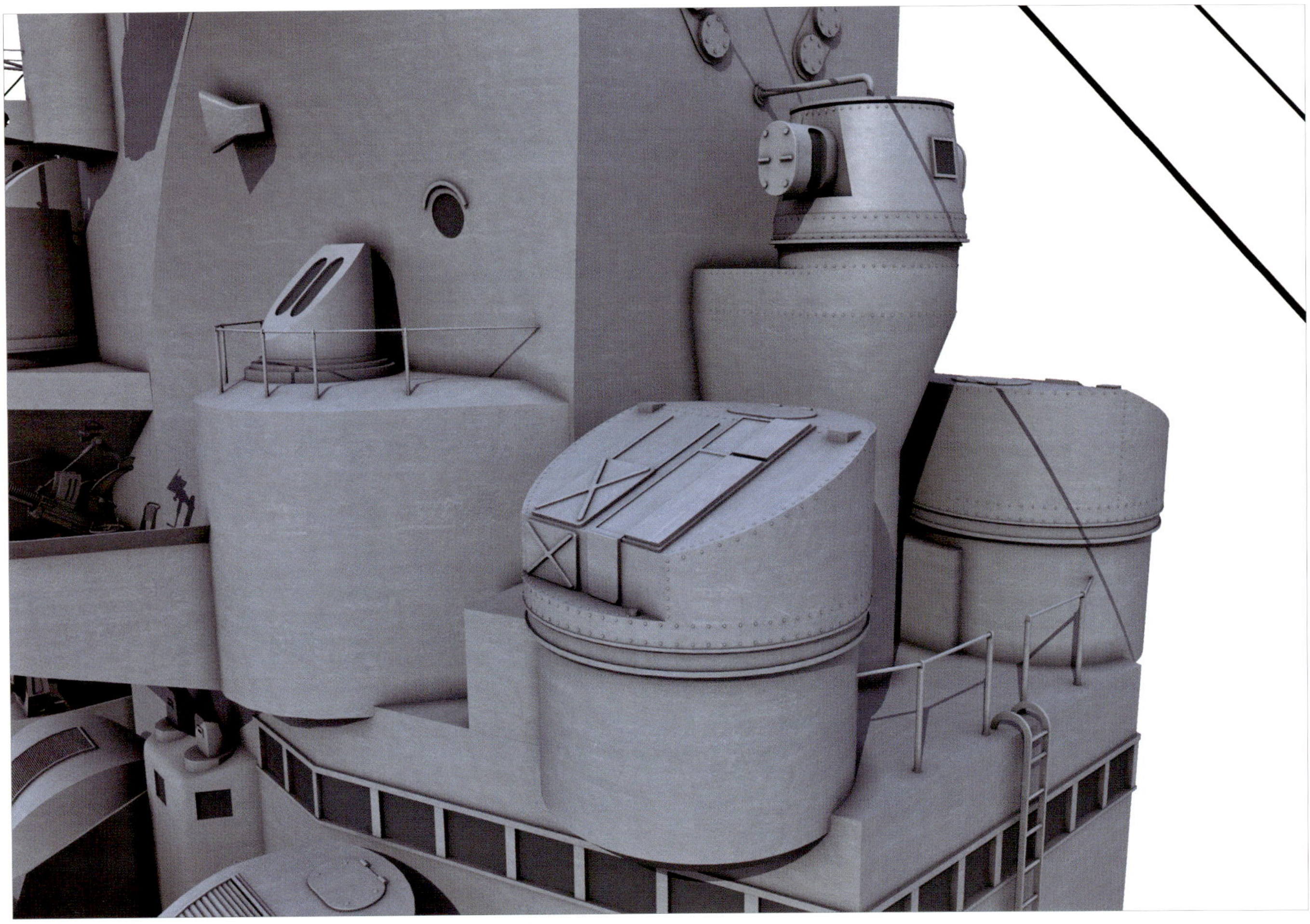

View of the Type 95 gun control tower from starboard side.

View of the front part of the conning tower from starboard side.

Overall view of the rear part of the battleship from portside.

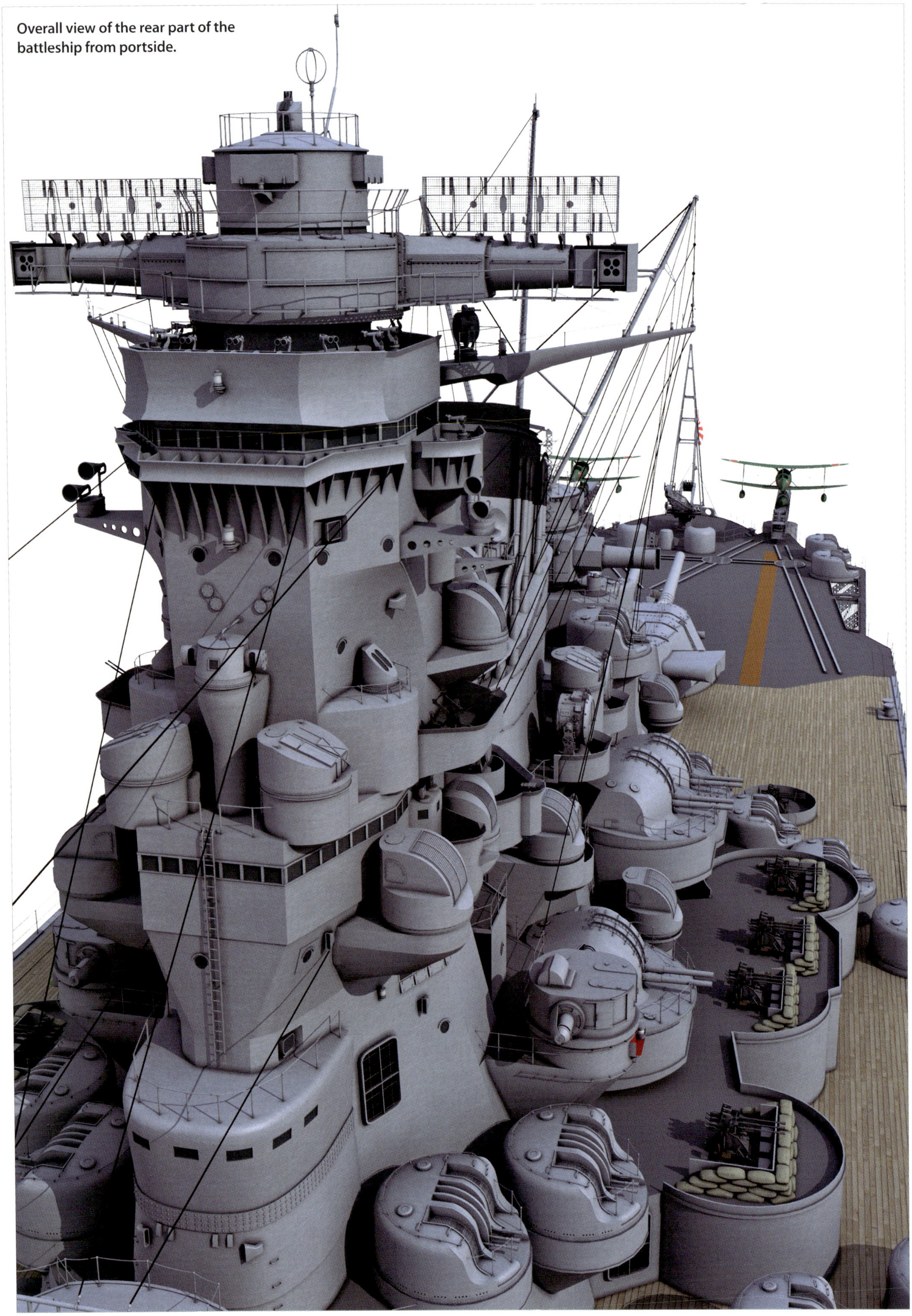

Overall view of the front part of the battleship from starboard side.

Back view of the 15 m rangefinder with Type 21 radar antennas.

Back view of the 15 m rangefinder and the rear lookouts.

Top view of the 15 m rangefinder.

View of the top of the tower bridge with the binoculars lookouts.

Close view of the 15 m rangefinder arm with the Type 21 radar antenna from port side.

The Type 21 radar antenna on port side.

Overall view of the rear part of the battleship from starboard side.

View of the wind intensity transmitter and wind direction indicator fitted on both arms on top of the tower bridge structure.

View of gun and searchlight control tower fitted at side of compass bridge starboard side. Note the 60 cm signal lamp on the starboard side.

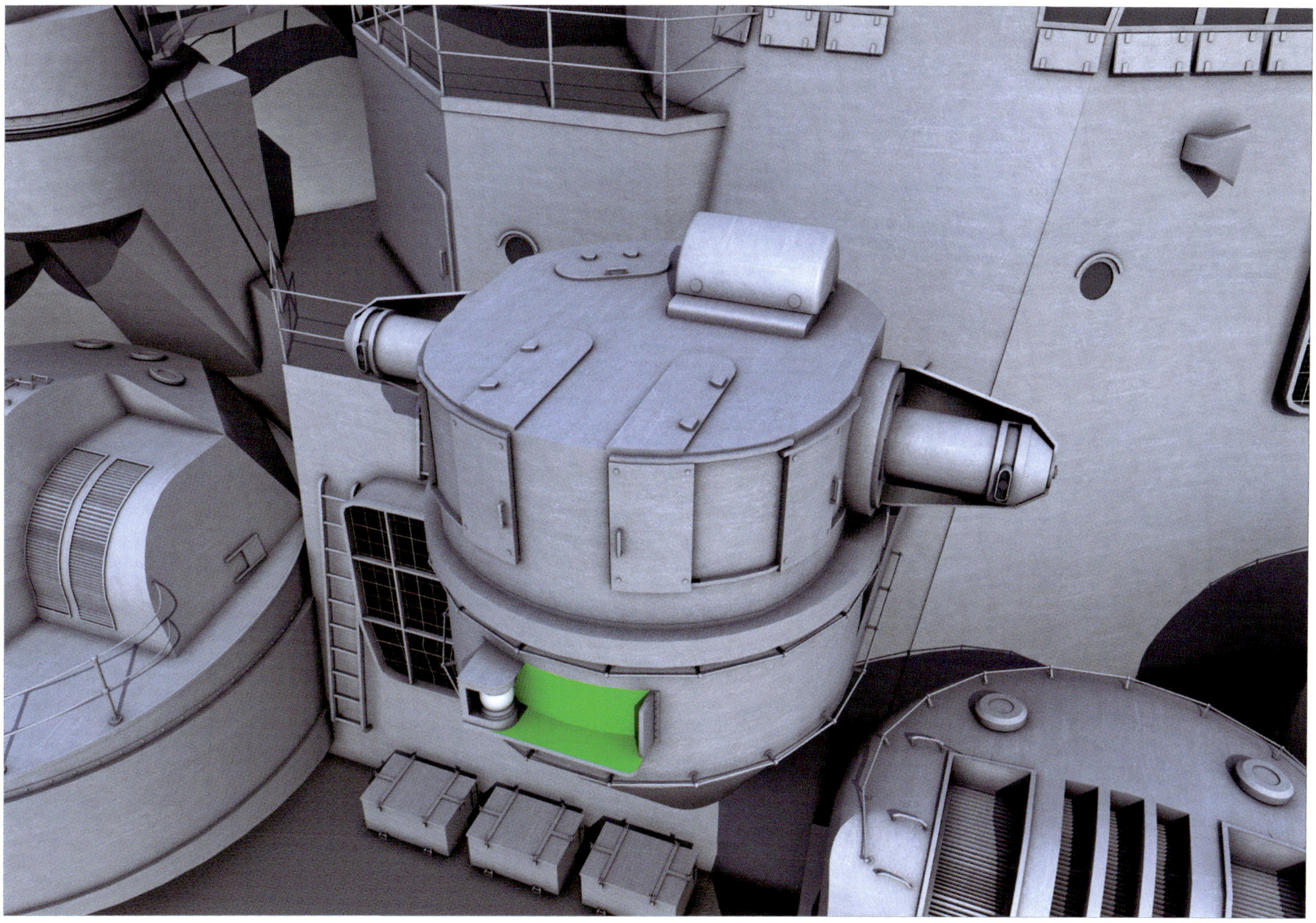

View of the 4.5 m Type 94 rangefinder with navigation light from starboard side.

View of the 4.5 m Type 94 rangefinder with navigation light from starboard side.

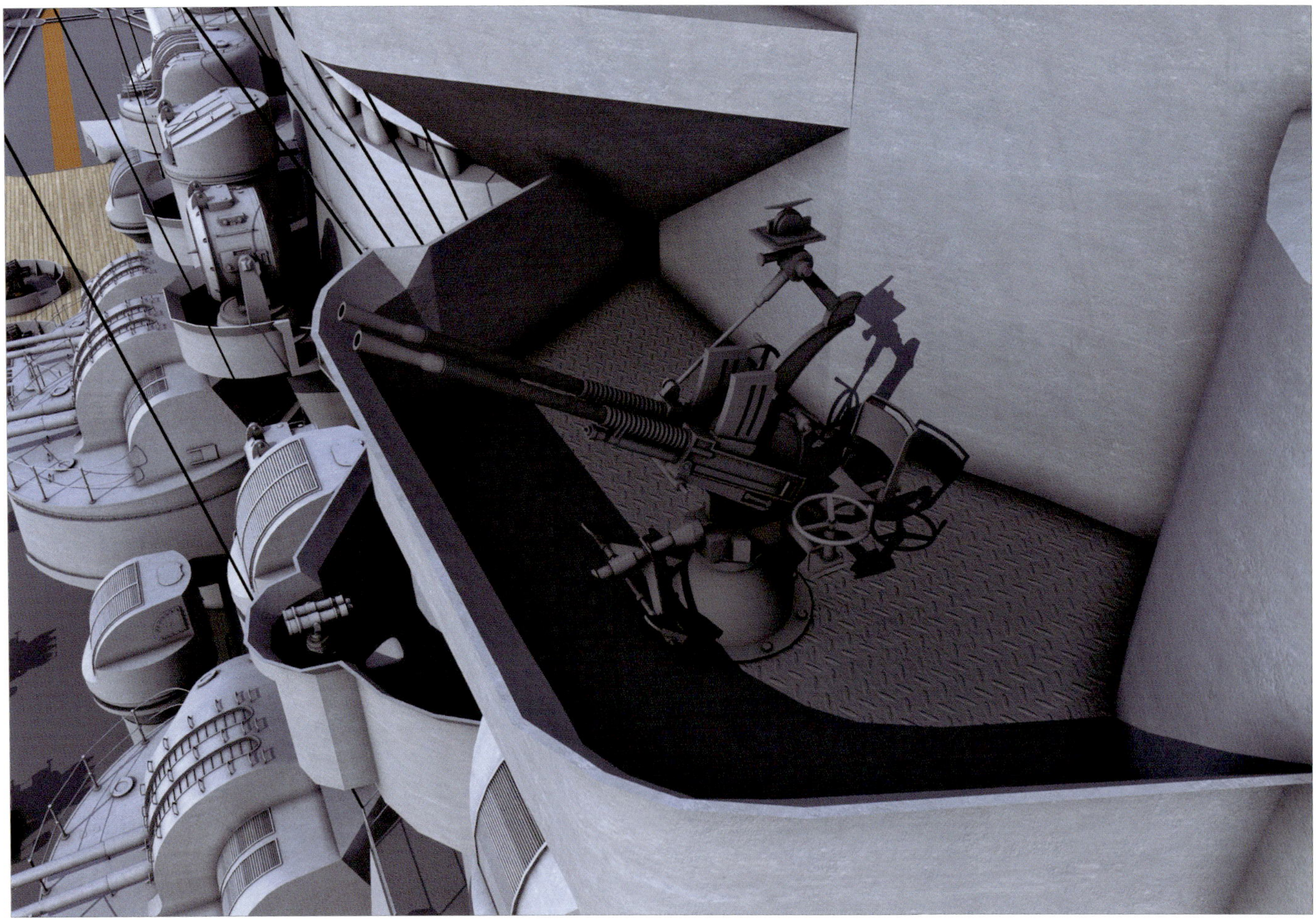

View of one 13 mm Type 93 "Shiki" Twin anti aircraft gun from starboard side.

View of one 12.7 cm Type 89 anti aircraft gun turret model A-1-3 from starboard side.

View of a gun control tower on starboard side.

Overall view of the rear of the conning tower.

Overall view of the front part of the battleship from starboard side.

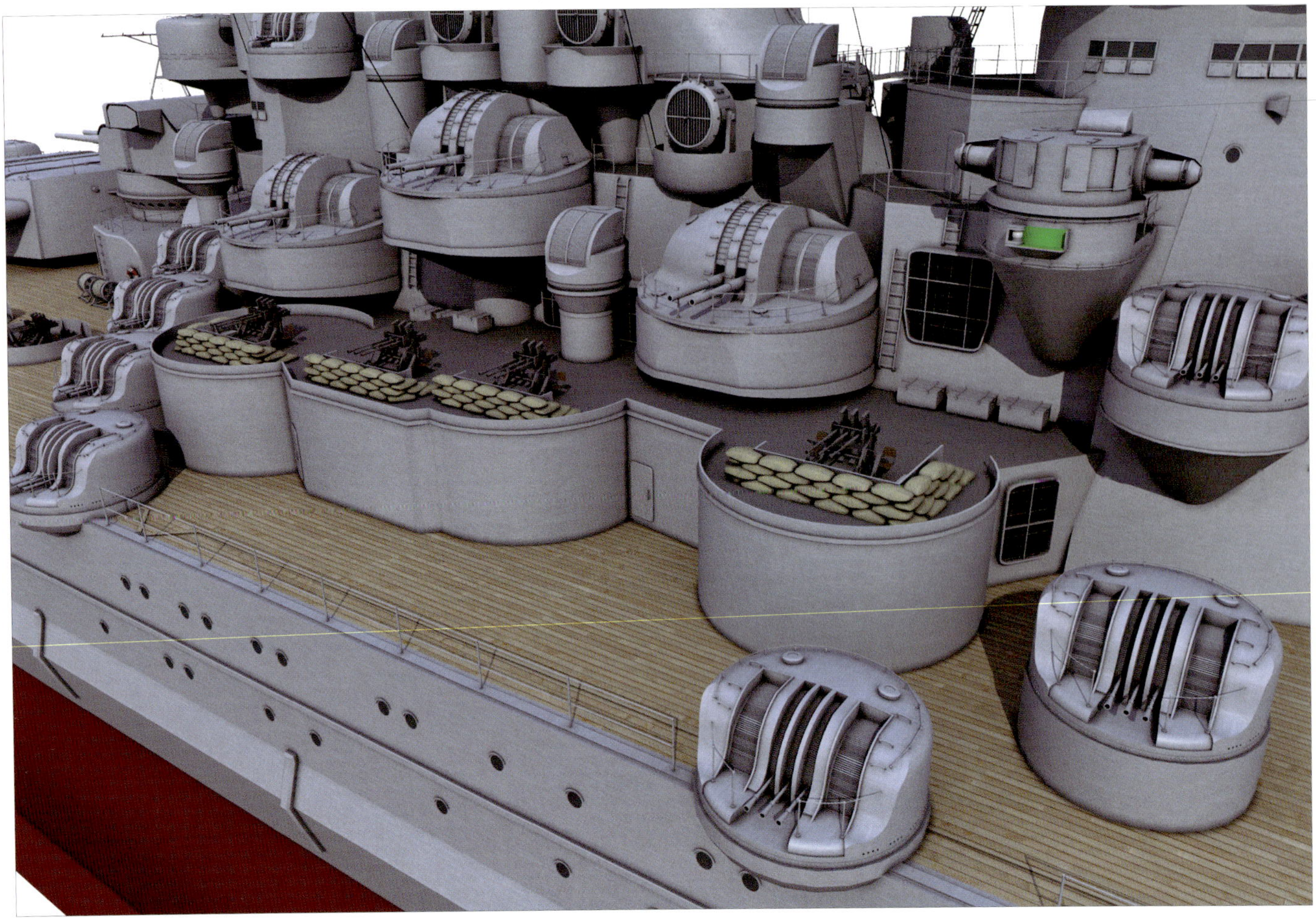

Anti aircraft batteries on starboard side.

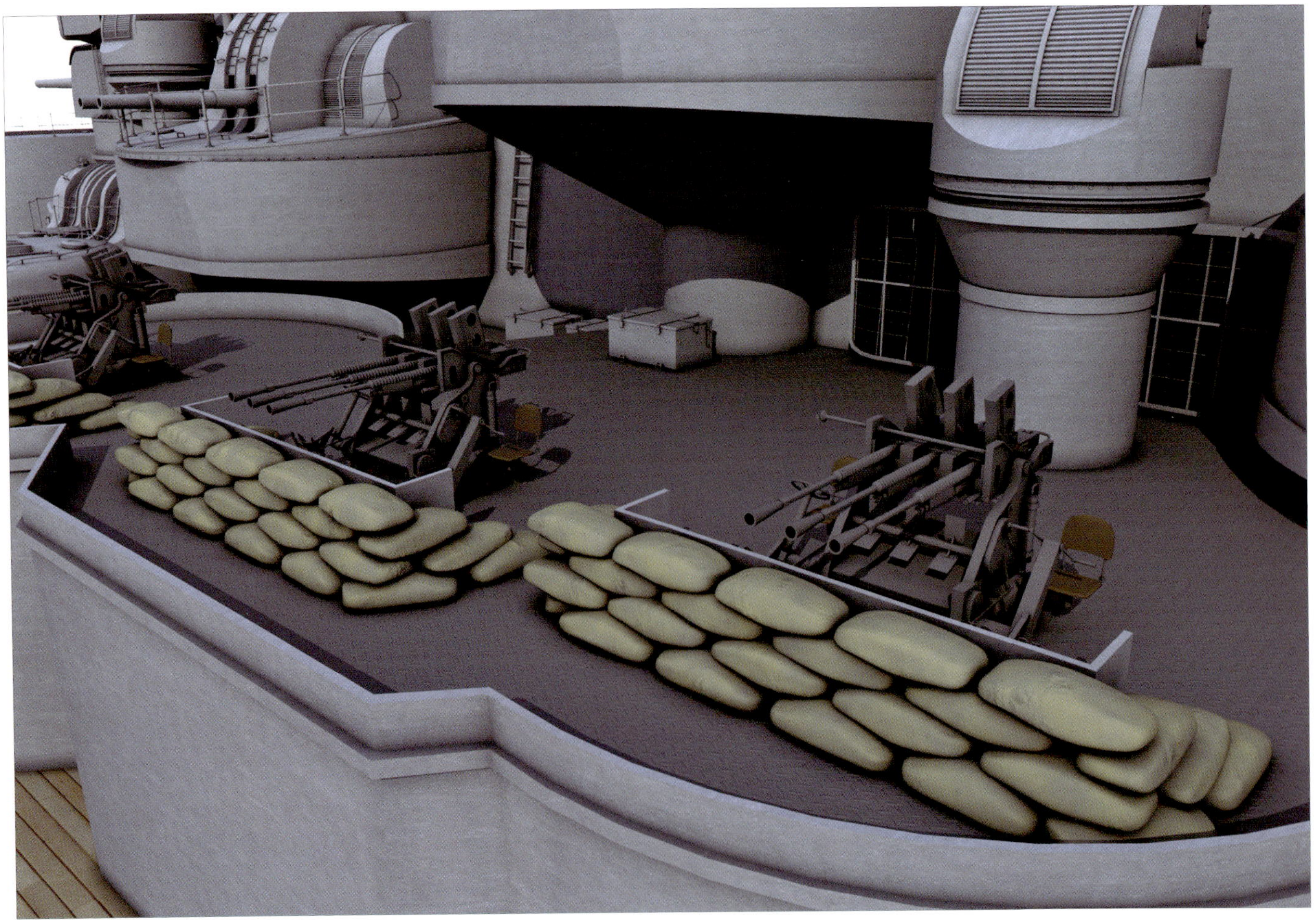

View of the Type 96 triple 25 mm anti aircraft gun on starboard side.

View of one 12.7 cm Type 89 anti aircraft gun turret model A-1-3 from starboard side.

View of the funnel.

View of the funnel area from starboard side.

▼ View of the top of the funnel from starboard side.

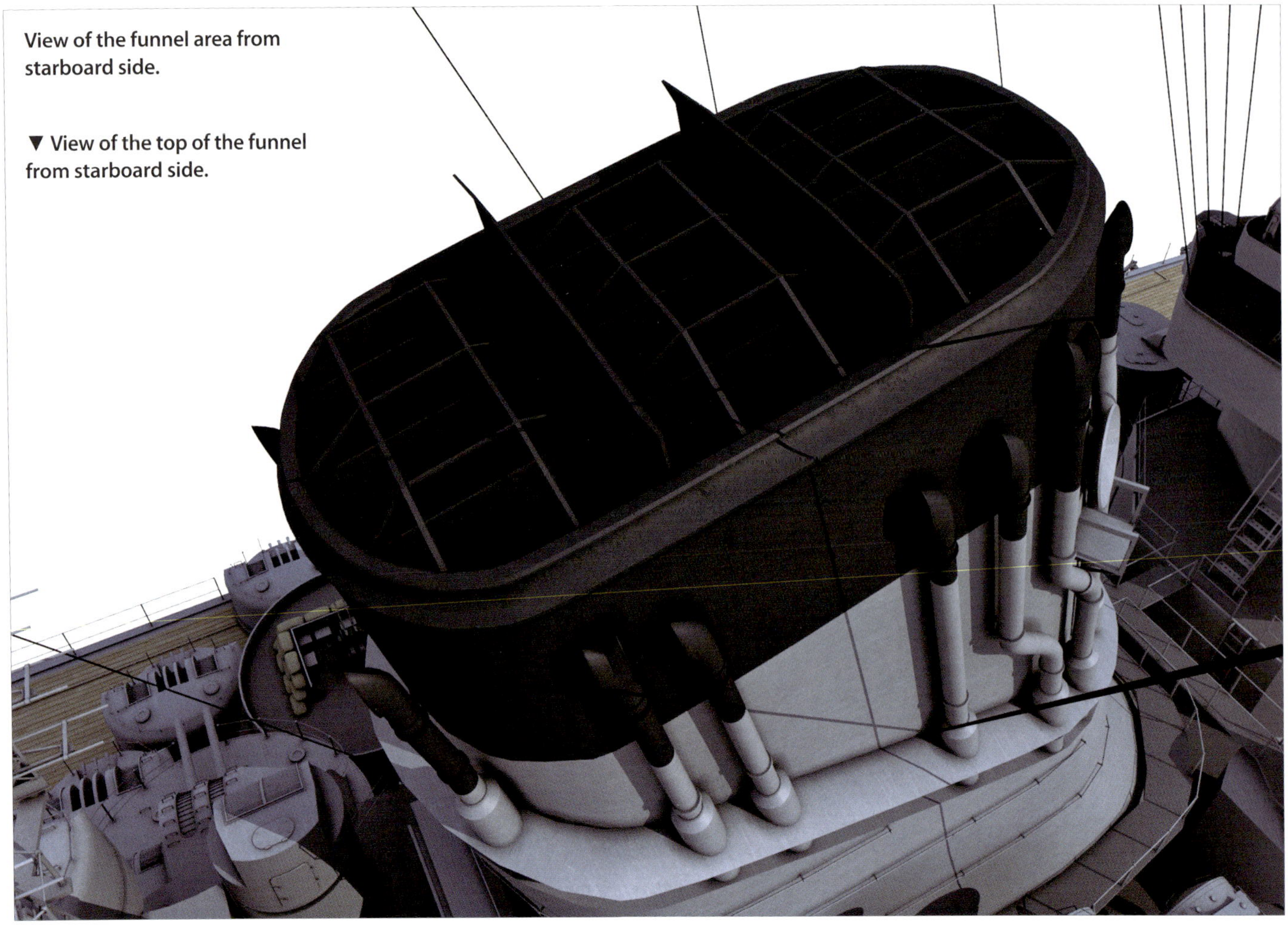

View of the 13 'GO' Type Air Search Radar Antenna.

View of Type 96 and Type 89 anti aircraft batteries from starboard side.

The anti aircraft batteries on port side.

Overall view of port side anti aircraft batteries.

View of one 12.7 cm Type 89 anti aircraft gun turret model A-1-3 from portside.

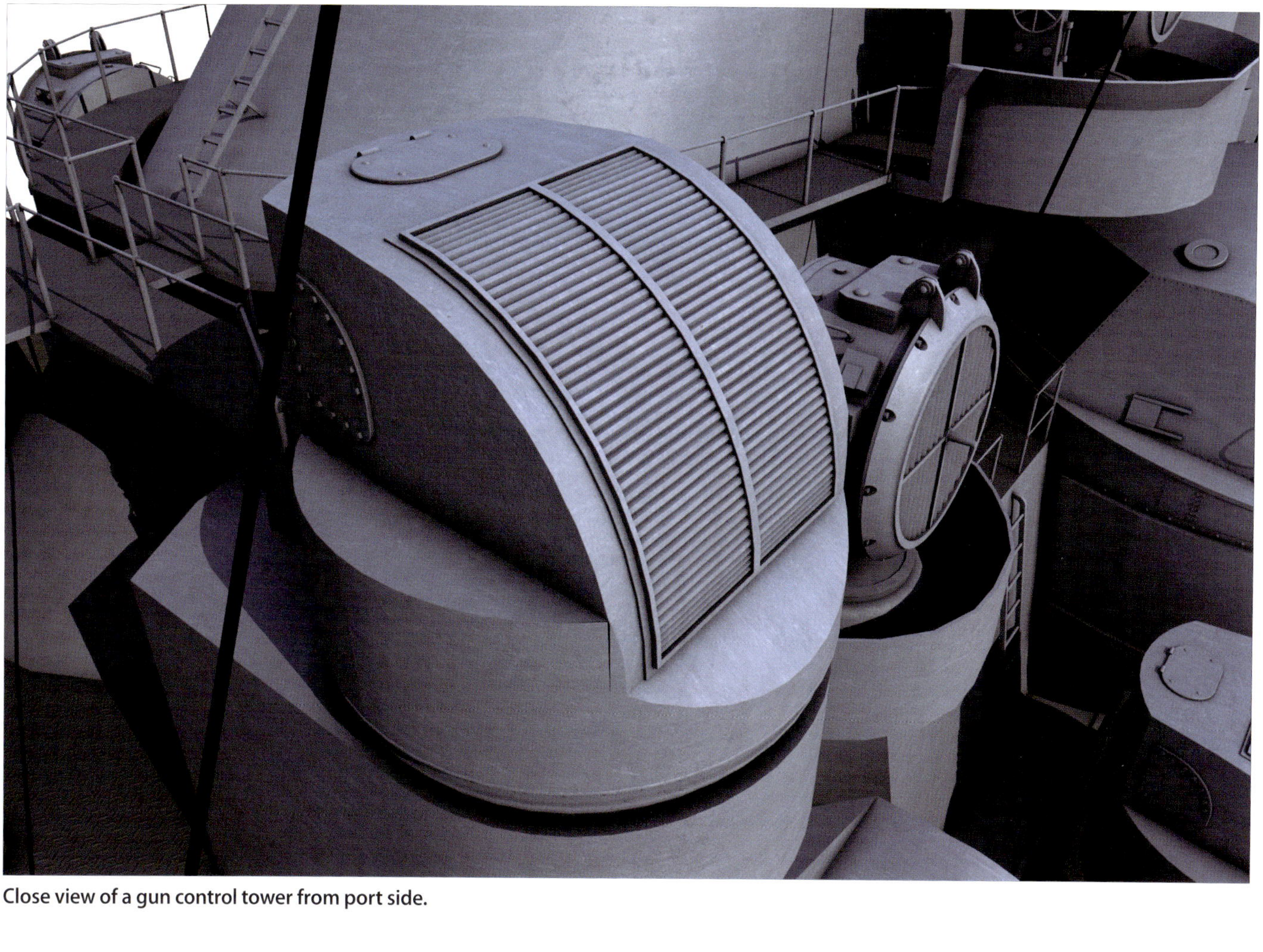

Close view of a gun control tower from port side.

View of gun and searchlight control tower fitted at side of compass bridge on port side.

Close view of the bottom of the conning tower from port side.

Close view of a 150 cm searchlight from port side.

Close view of a 150 cm searchlight from port side.

View of one Type 96 triple 25 mm anti aircraft gun on starboard side.

View of one Type 96 triple 25 mm anti aircraft gun on starboard side. Note the scupper to carry water overboard from the deck.

Overall view of the tripod main mast.

Overall view of the main mast.

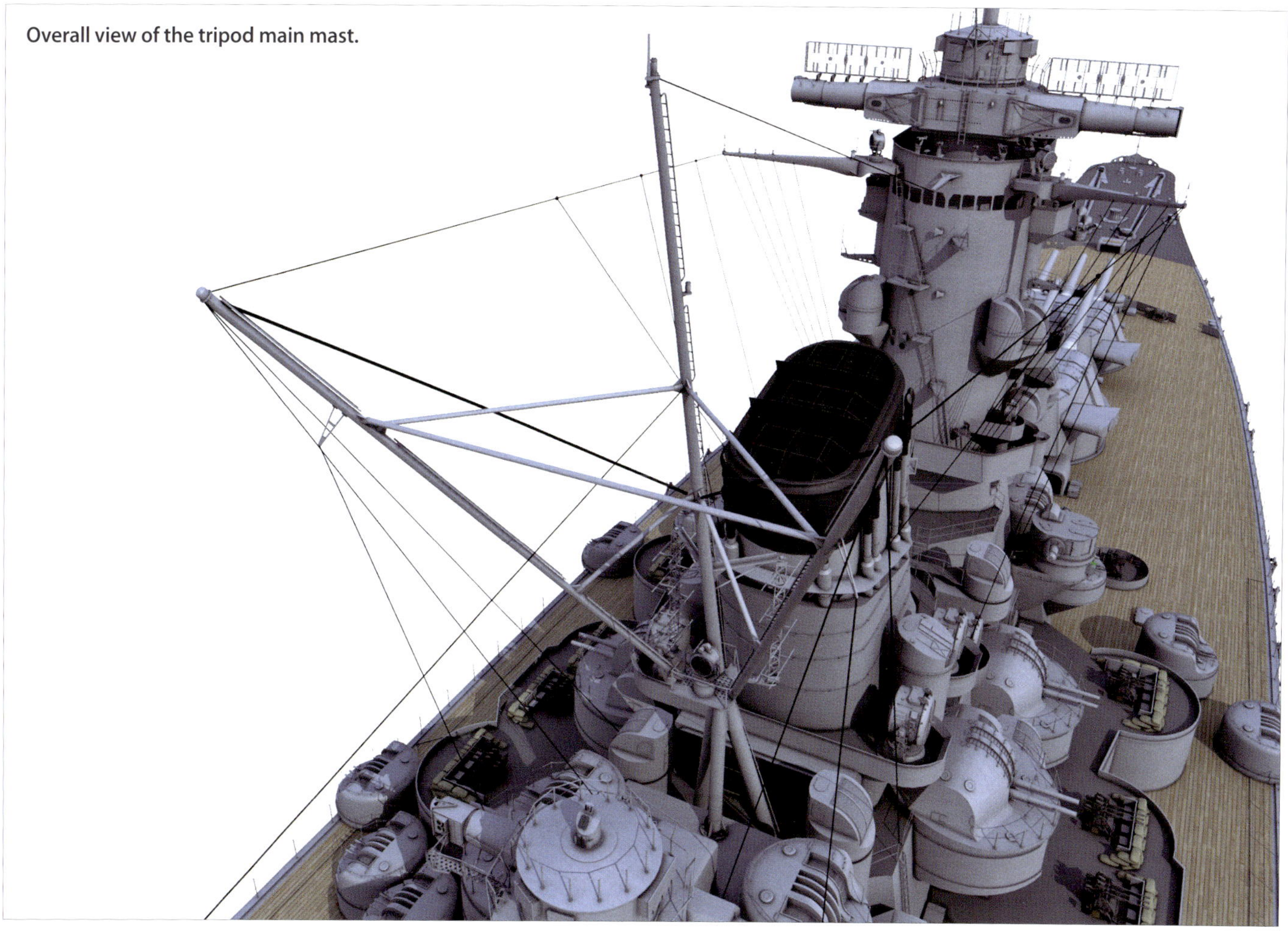

Overall view of the tripod main mast.

View of the 10 m rangefinder with two Type 96 triple 25 mm guns aft.

View of the 10 m rangefinder.

View of the 10 m rangefinder.

Overall view of the main mast.

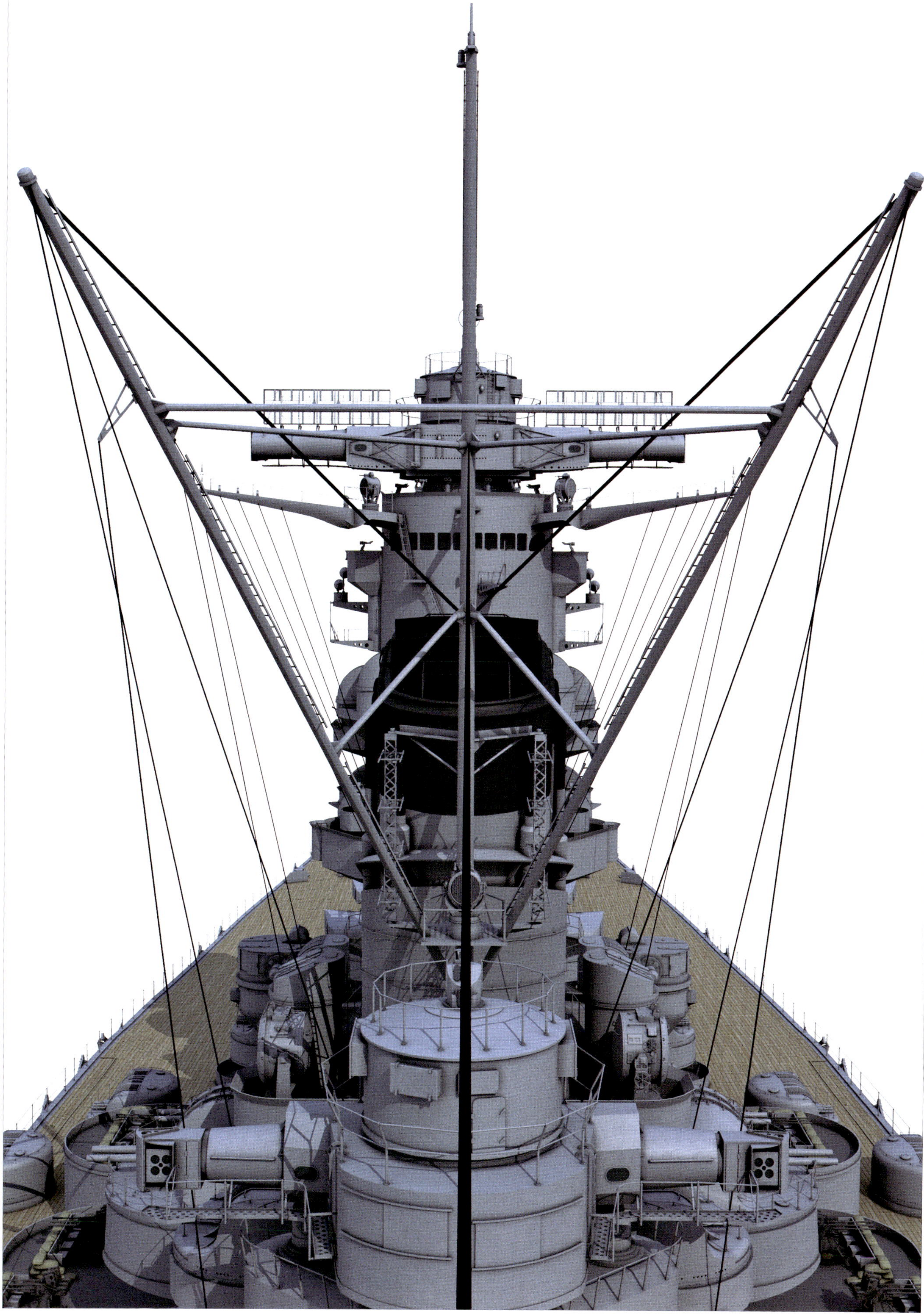

Top view of the 10 m rangefinder.

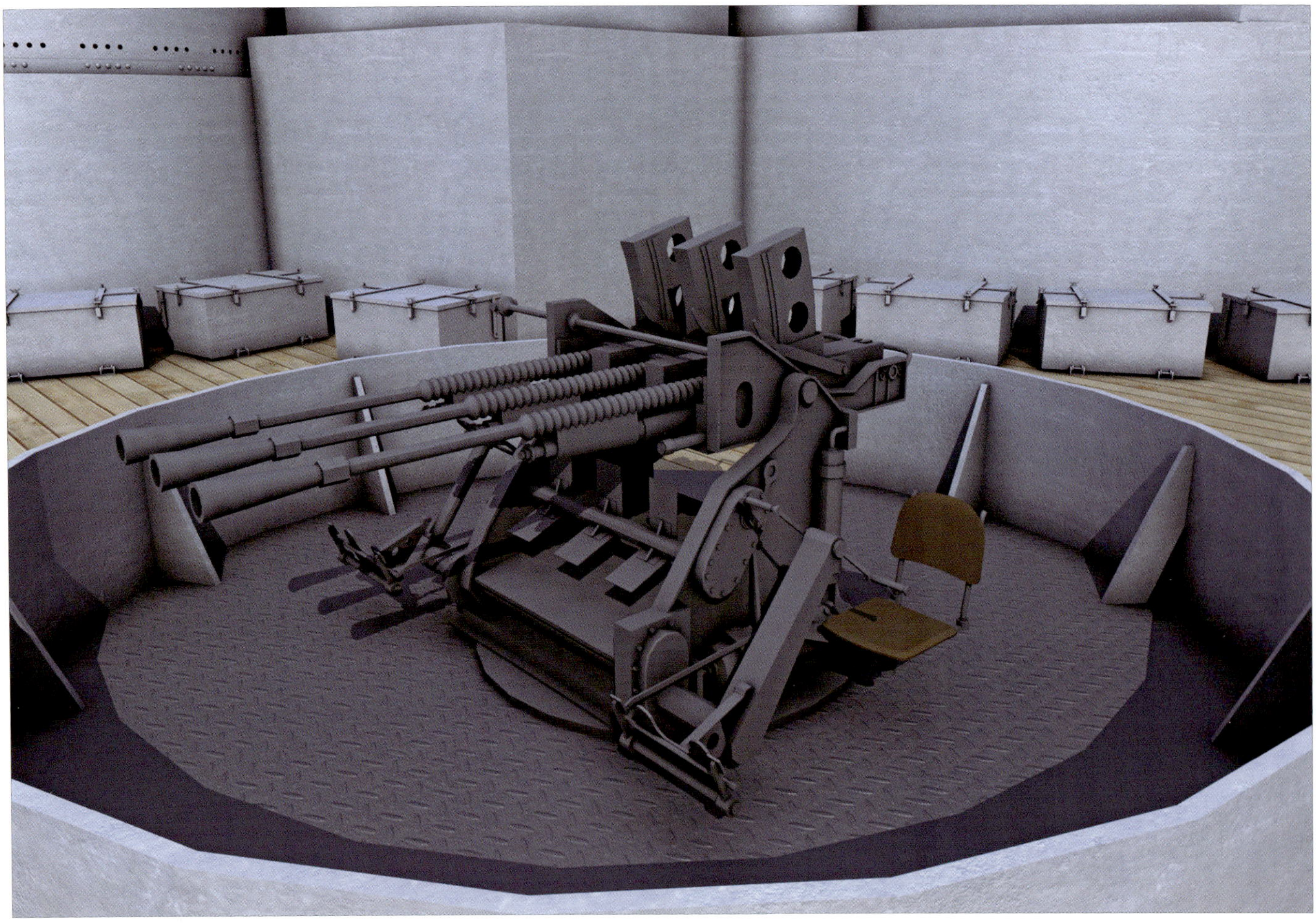

Close view of a Type 96 triple 25 mm anti aircraft gun fitted on port side.

Close view of a Type 96 triple 25 mm anti aircraft gun fitted on port side.

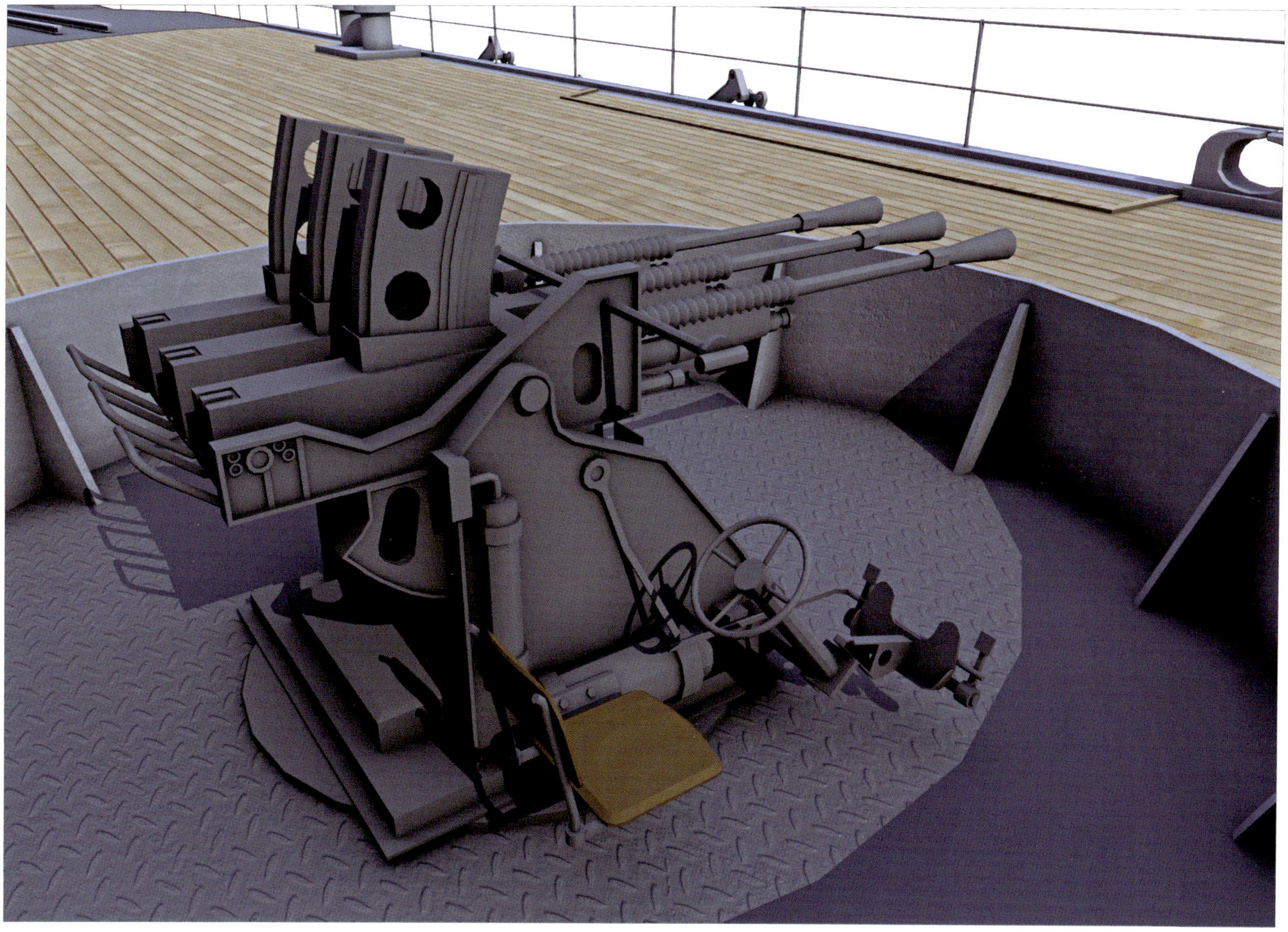

Overall view of the 10 m rangefinder area with ventilators.

View of the 15.5 cm turret 'Nendo Shiki' No. 2.

View of the 15.5 cm turret 'Nendo Shiki' No. 2.

View of the 15.5 cm turret basement with ventilators.

View of two Type 96 'Shiki' triple 25 mm AA gun aft.

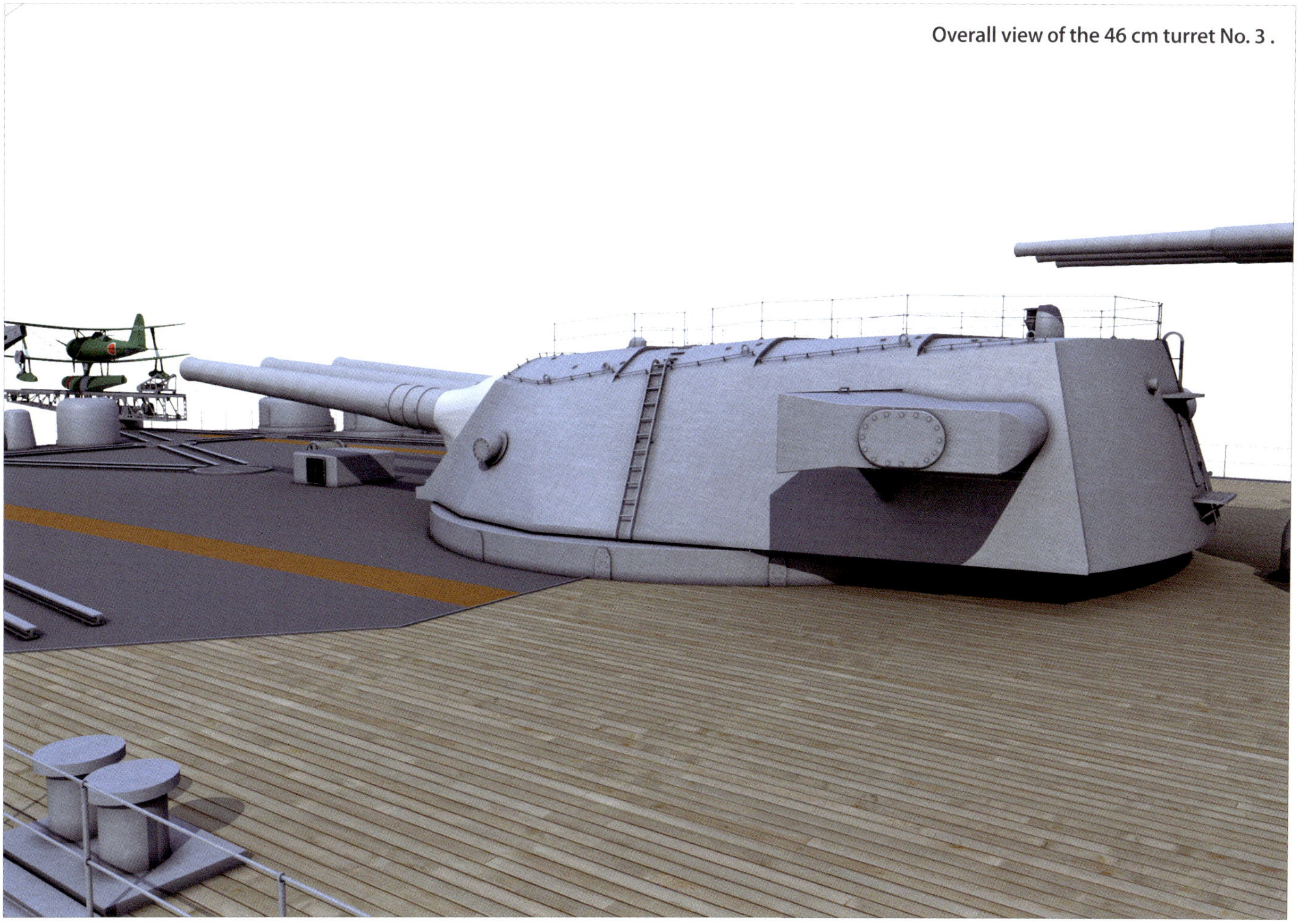
Overall view of the 46 cm turret No. 3 .

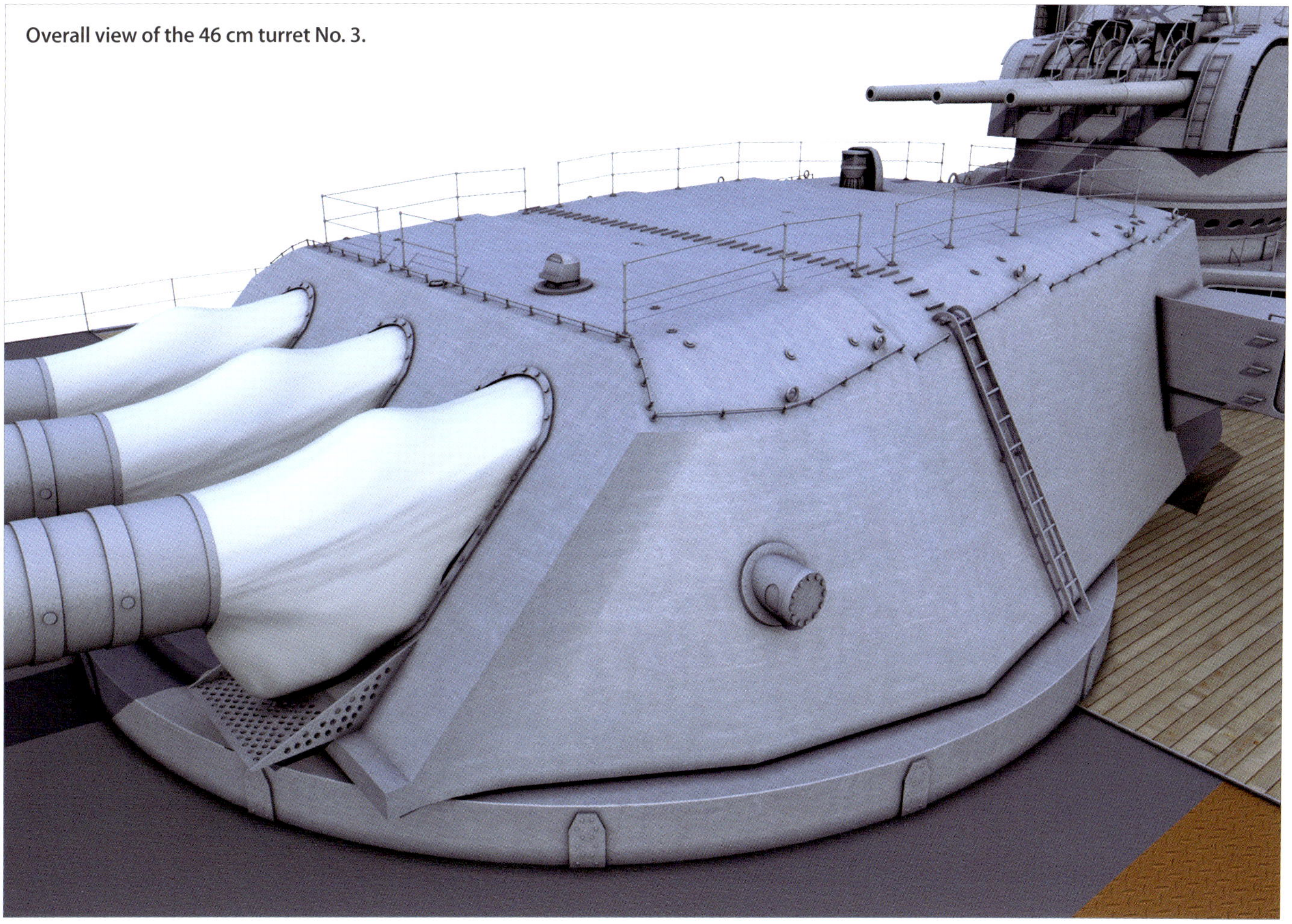
Overall view of the 46 cm turret No. 3.

View of the 15.5 cm turret 'Nendo Shiki' No. 2 and 10 m rangefinder from the top of the 46 cm turret No. 3.

Overall view of the 46 cm turret No. 3 from the stern.

Overall view of the 46 cm turret No. 3 from starboard side.

View of other two Type 96 'Shiki' triple 25 mm AA gun aft from starboard side.

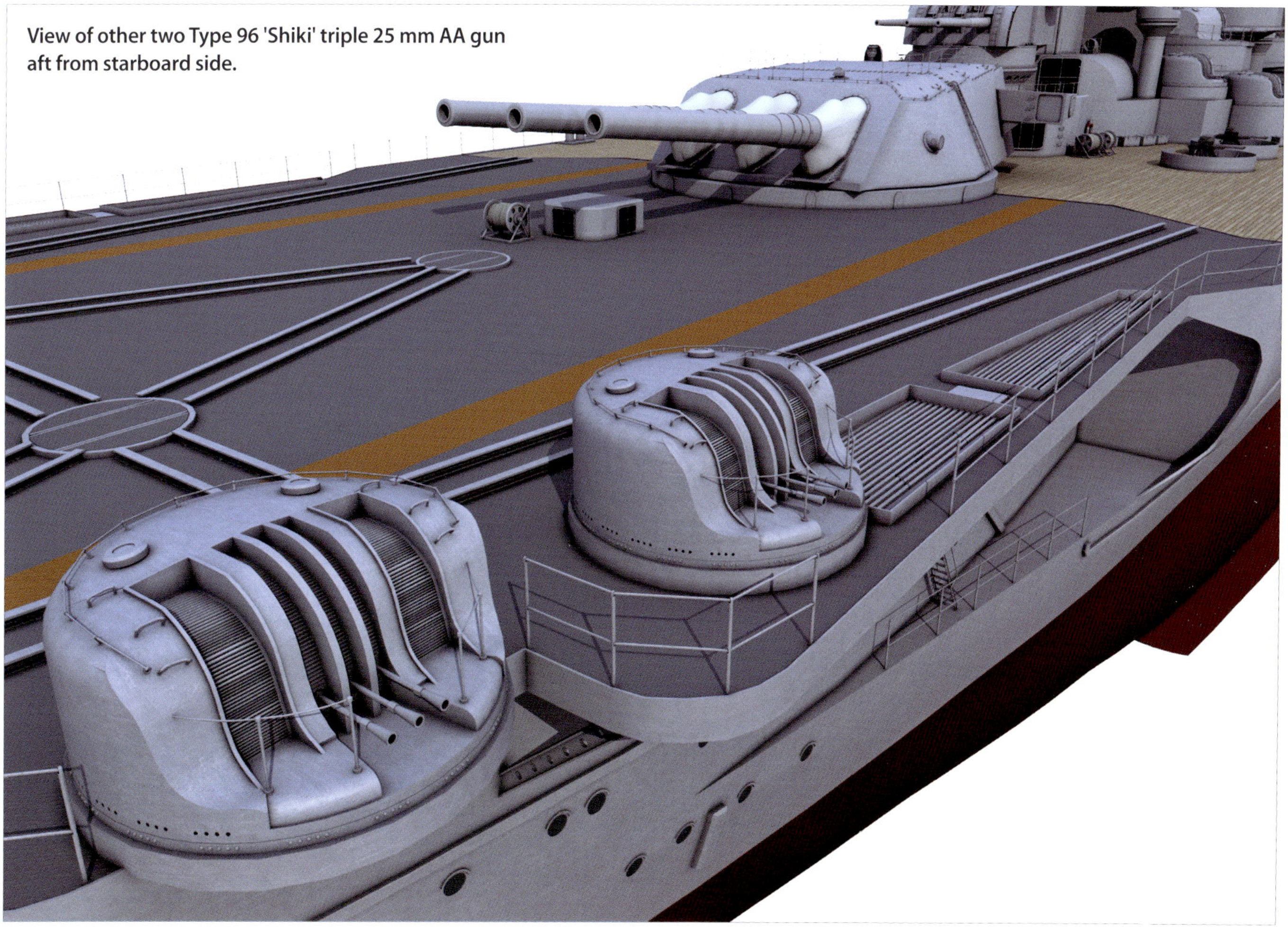

Aircraft deck from port side.

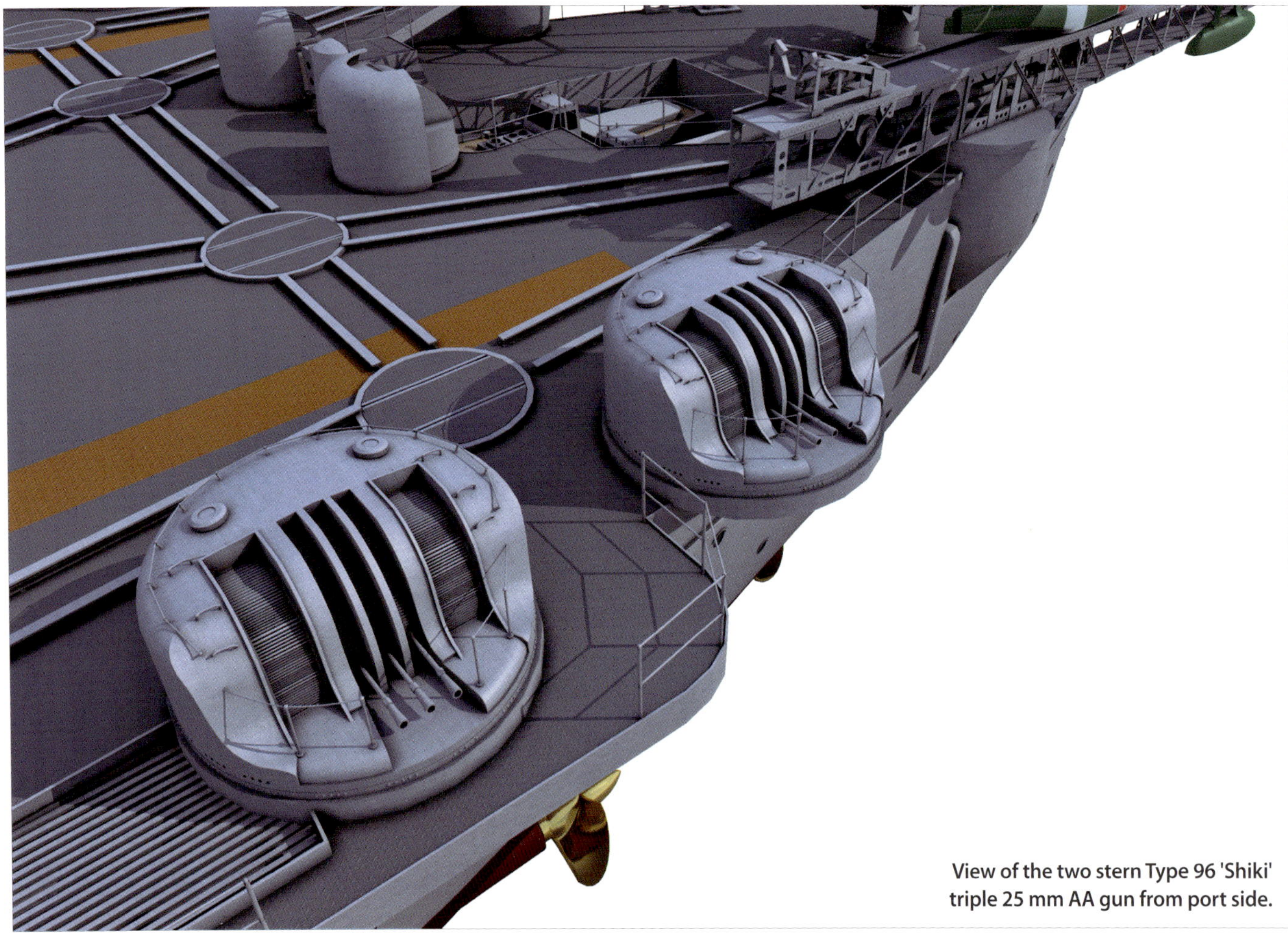

View of the two stern Type 96 'Shiki' triple 25 mm AA gun from port side.

Structures on the aircraft deck.

Overall view of the 46 cm turret No. 3 from port side. Note the ventilators below the guns.

View of structures aft from starboard side.

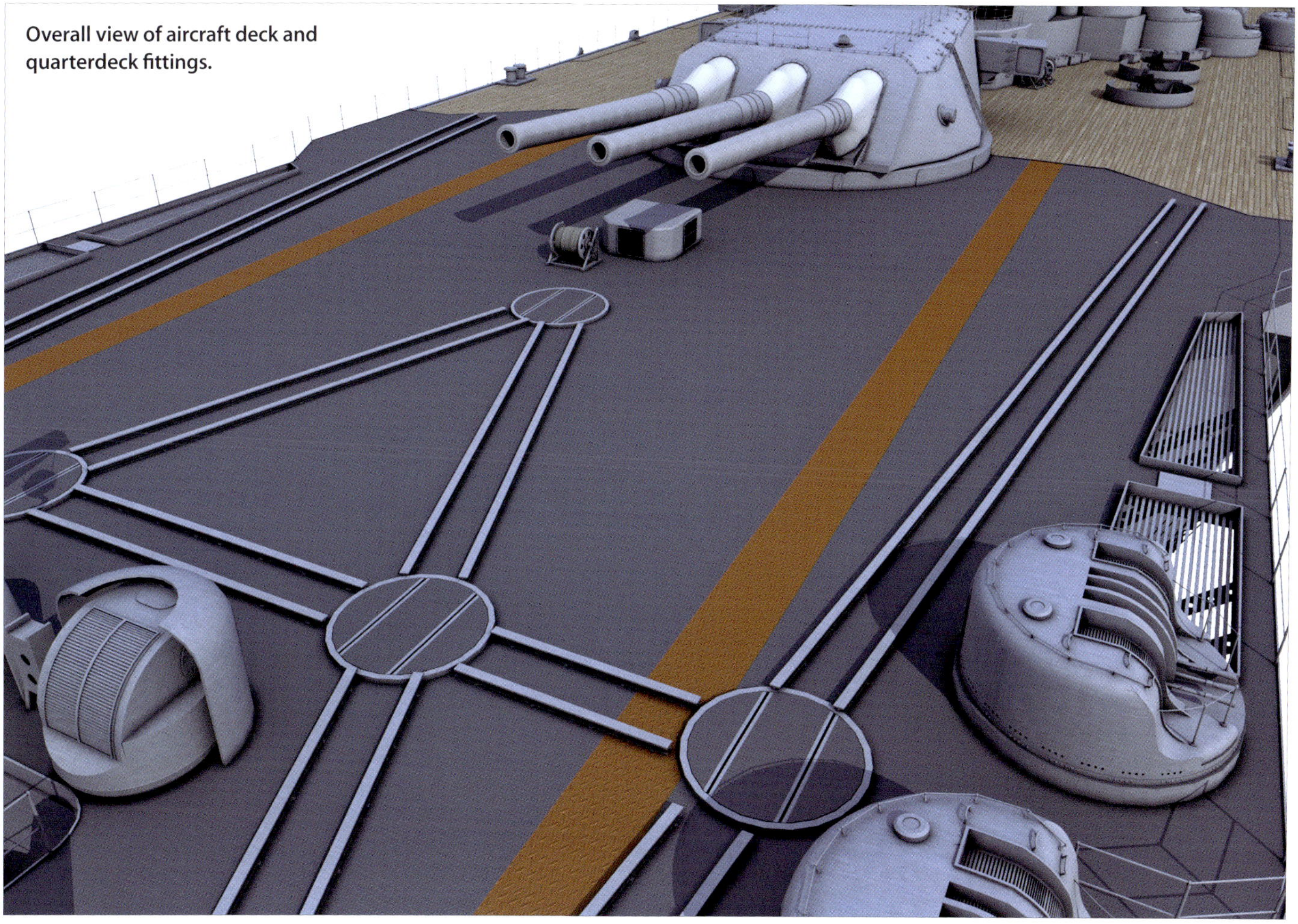

Overall view of aircraft deck and quarterdeck fittings.

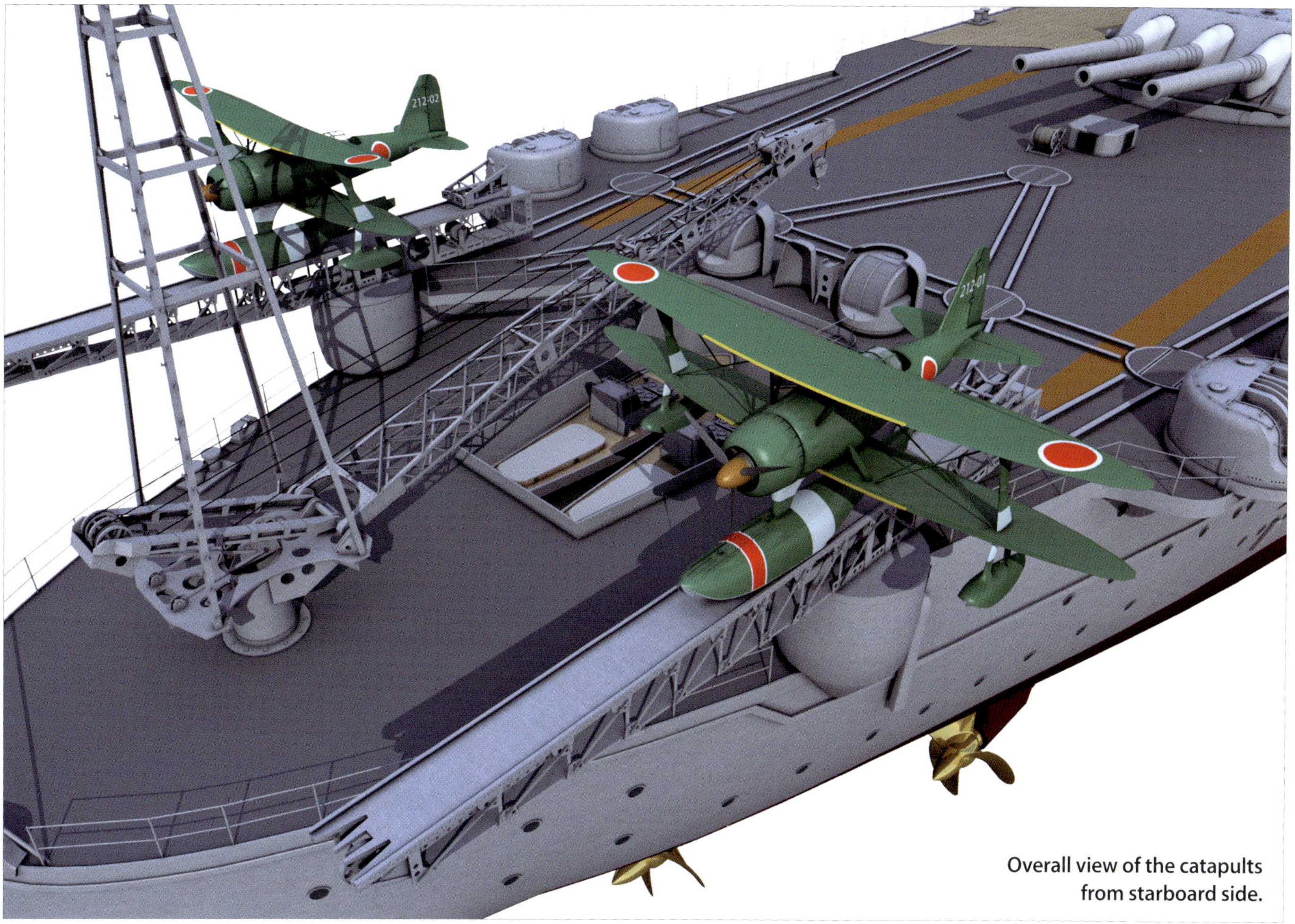

Overall view of the catapults from starboard side.

Overall view of portside catapult.

Overall view of the 6-ton stern crane.

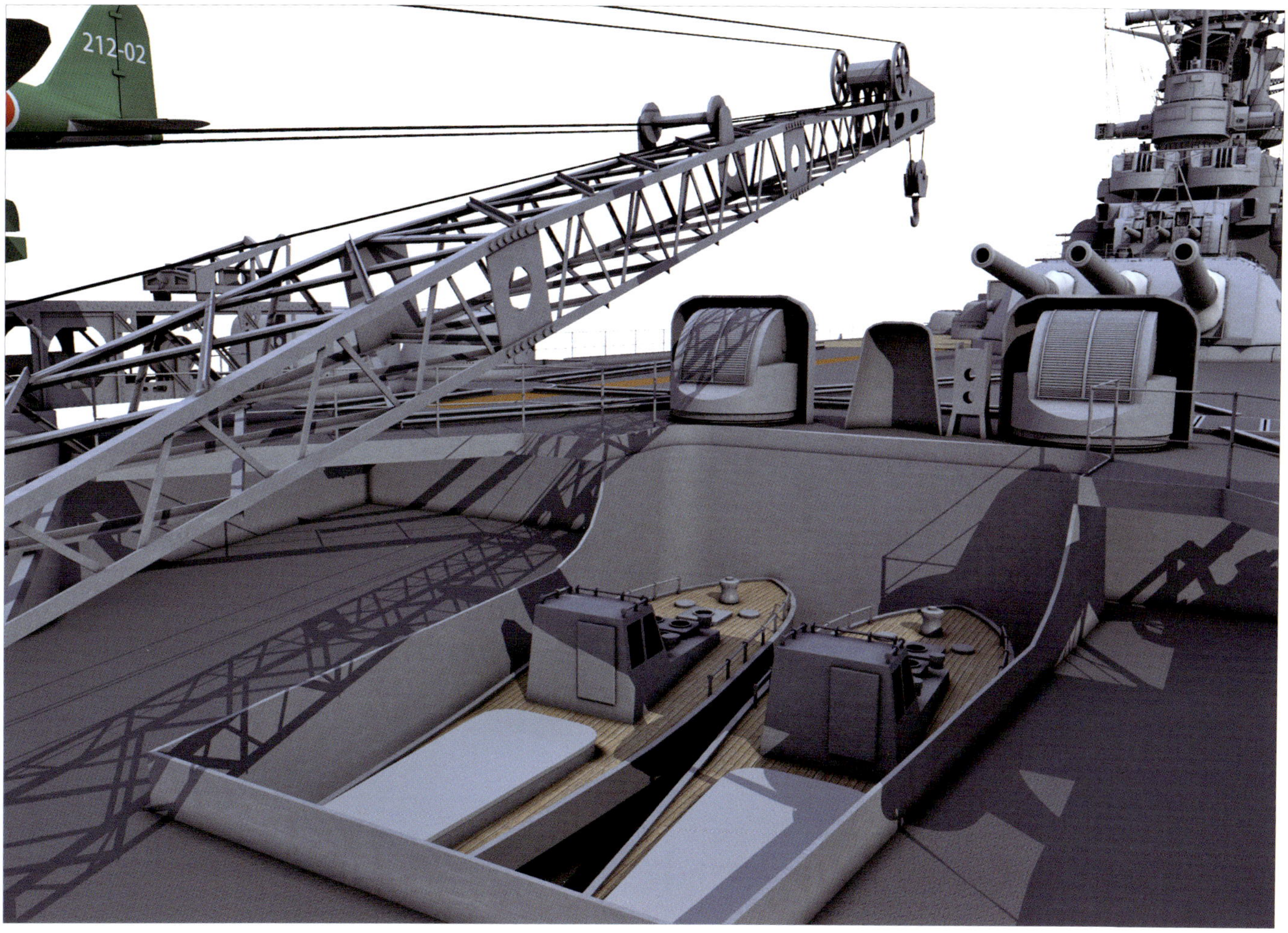

Overall view of the 6-ton stern crane (for aircraft and boats) with 15 m antenna mast.

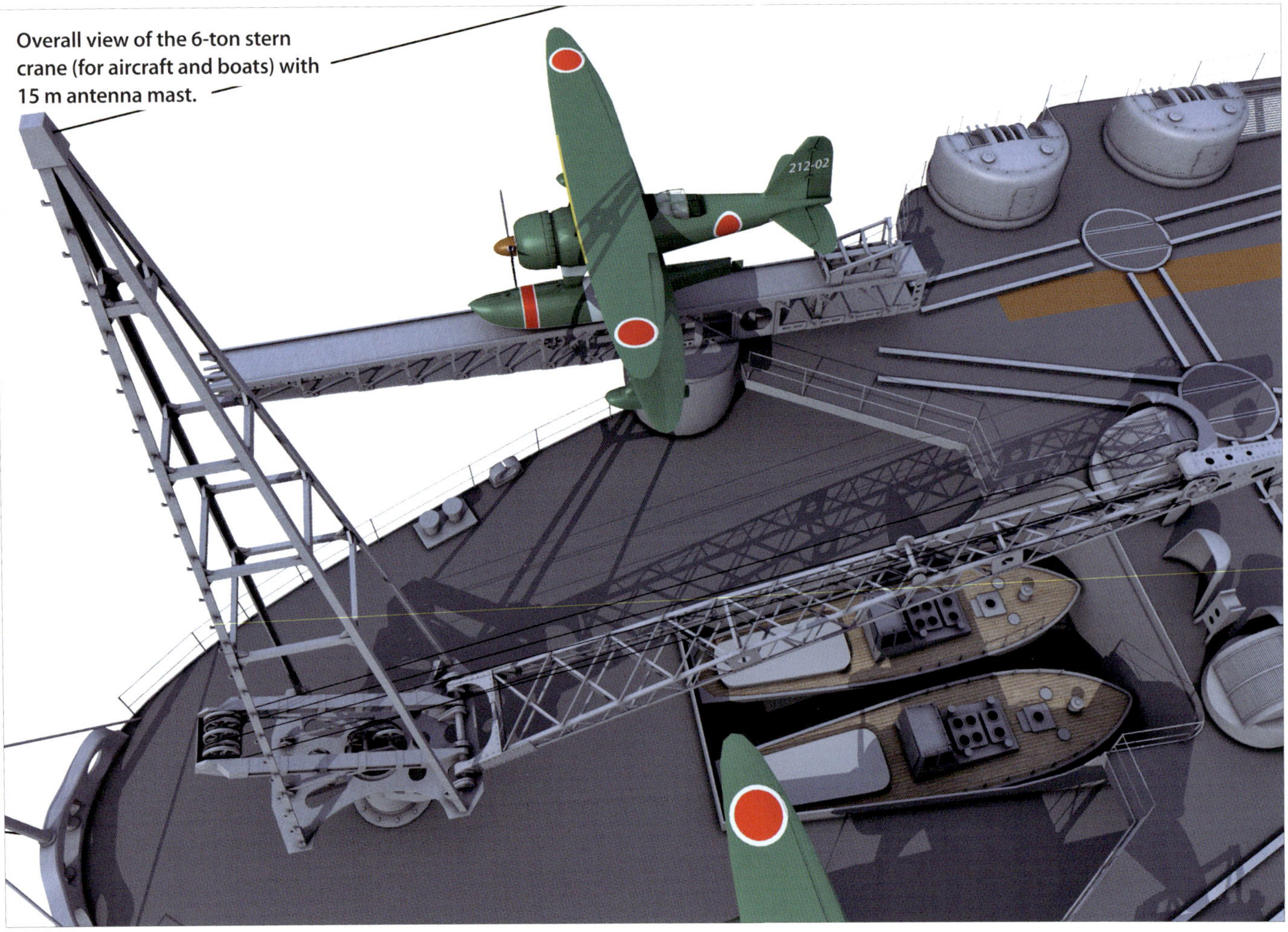

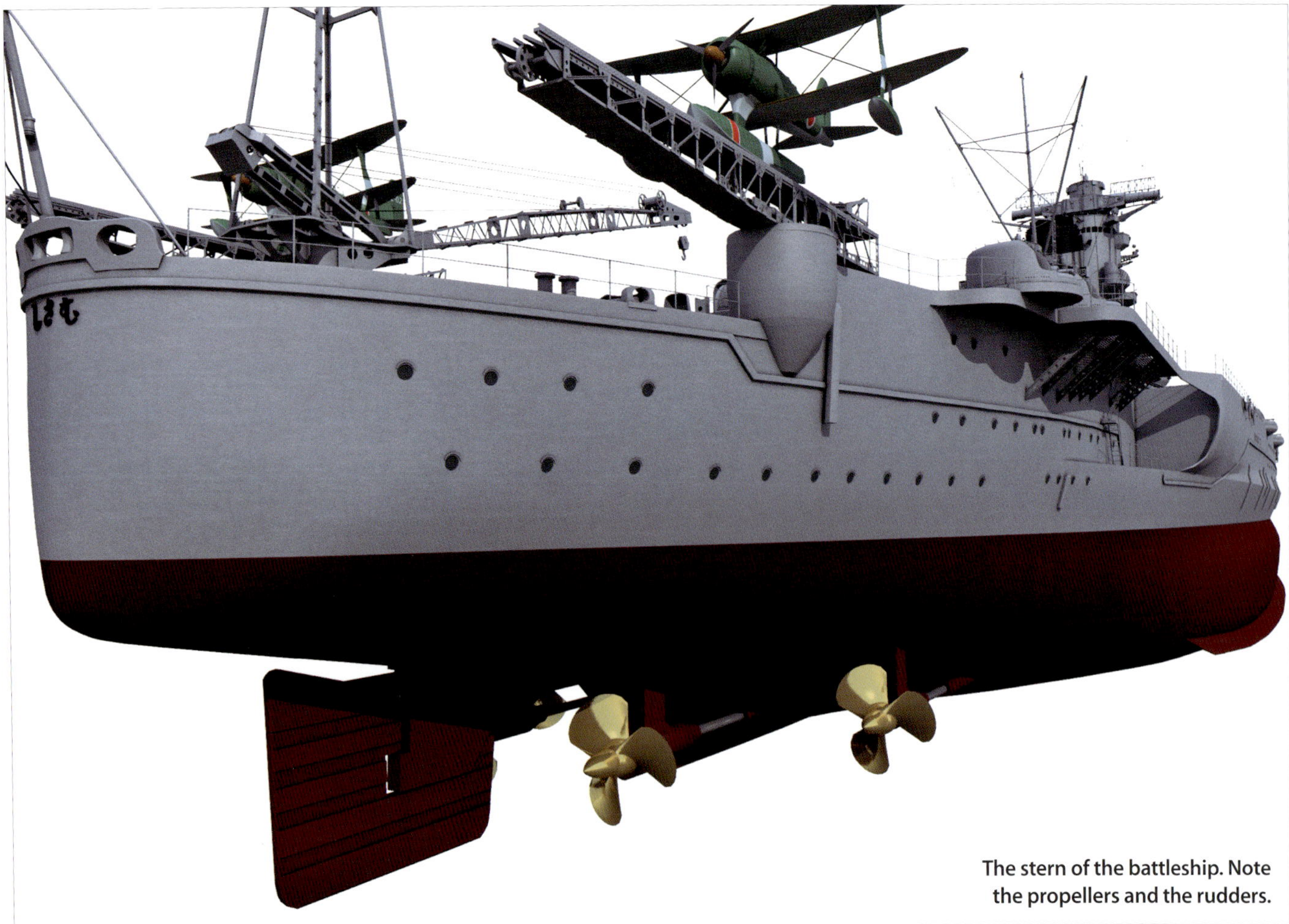

The stern of the battleship. Note the propellers and the rudders.

Overall view of the 6-ton stern crane with 15 m antenna mast.

The stern of the battleship with *Musashi* name.

The stern with the catapults and the 6-ton crane from port side.

View of the port side catapult.

The Japanese Battleship *Musashi* – Carlo Cestra
LUBLIN 2016 • ISBN 978-83-65437-23-5

3D illustrations, text and captions: **Carlo Cestra** • Design: **KAGERO STUDIO** – Marcin Wachowicz
Oficyna Wydawnicza KAGERO • www.kagero.pl, e-mail: kagero@kagero.pl, marketing@kagero.pl
Editorial office, Marketing, Distribution: KAGERO Publishing, Akacjowa 100, os. Borek, Turka, 20-258 Lublin 62, Poland, phone/fax (+48) 81 501 21 05
w w w . k a g e r o . e u